Life-Minded

—— The ——
Bible Study

*Intentional Practices for
Belonging to God and Each Other*

Brady Boyd

Our Daily Bread
Publishing.

ISBN: 978-1-64070-342-1

Printed in the United States of America
24 25 26 27 28 29 30 31 / 8 7 6 5 4 3 2 1

Contents

Before We Begin

Welcome to *Life-Minded, The Bible Study*! I'm thrilled you've decided to dig into such a critical topic for our age, that of unity, not only in the world at large but more specifically within the church.

I've pastored New Life Church in Colorado Springs, Colorado, for sixteen years now, but I hail originally from the enchanting land of Louisiana, renowned for wild parades, live jazz, a natural landscape marked by bayous and swamps, and locals who know how to say the plural of *y'all*. And then there's the cooking. If you've never savored Cajun or Creole eats, in my humble estimation you just haven't lived. They're delectable. They're distinctive. And they're *addictive* like no other fare.

I bring this up because when I think about the subject of unity, I think of one of my favorite Louisiana dishes: *gumbo*. Gumbo is a beautiful blend of diverse ingredients—a nice thick roux, some rough-chopped mirepoix (back home we call it the "holy trinity," but don't hold that against me), chicken stock, herbs and spices, some tomatoes, a few glugs of hot sauce, and whichever protein you prefer (shrimp is a must, chicken and andouille are optional, oysters are a definite no-no). Together they yield a fantastic dish. Let that filled-to-the-brim stockpot simmer on low for a few hours, boil some rice just before mealtime, and prepare to be wowed. *Delicious.*

Christian unity works the same way.

Combine heartfelt devotion to God, a handful of acts of service, a pinch of conversational curiosity, a dash of discernment in using your words wisely, and generous helpings of things like peacefulness, forgiveness, grace, and awe, and the fragrance that will waft through your home, your community, your city, and your world will leave your senses utterly undone. That's what we're here to do: to prioritize unity. To sharpen the practices that encourage unity to unfold in our midst. And to trust God to equip us day by day to be the unifiers we're made to be.

I hope you love the sessions to come as much as I loved putting them together for you. The practices you're about to experiment with come straight from Scripture and therefore can be wholly trusted to grow you into the image of God, the *ultimate* unifier. May he bless and keep you as you both seek to know him more intimately as a result of this study and seek increasingly to make him known.

Rooting for you as you live like Jesus—

Brady Boyd
January 2024
Colorado Springs

Preparing for the Journey Ahead

Session Setup

You don't have to look far to find evidence that divisiveness—disunity—is alive and (unfortunately) well in our world today. We are experiencing unparalleled political polarization, ideological warfare, and the seeming inability of government officials to get along. We are experiencing deeply rooted cultural conflicts, reflected by the rise of activist groups and online debates that grow only more venomous over time. We are experiencing a wild uptick in the creation and spread of misinformation and disinformation, propagated at lightning speed over social media. The net effect of these and other trends is a level of collective rage and resulting division many of us have never seen in our lifetimes.

It's a grim scene. But it doesn't exist in a vacuum. Because just as plentiful evidence exists that disunity is having a real moment right now, plentiful evidence exists that every tool we need for *building unity* is right here in our hands.

Opener

Before you screen this session's video, share your thoughts on the following questions.

What is one daily practice you wouldn't want to live without, and why?

When was the last time you incorporated a new practice into your daily life, and why did you choose it?

 ## Video Notes

As you watch the video, log impactful phrases or key takeaways based on the prompts below.

The usefulness of a crossroads

The devastating drift

We play like we practice

An easy guarantee

Why it's dark, and why we're light

Group Discussion

Work through the following questions in full group, addressing as many as time and interest permit.

1. When have you experienced a spiritual watershed moment like the one described in the video?

2. Do you agree or disagree that the light we bring to the world because of Jesus living inside of us is the answer to the pervasive darkness we see? Why?

3. What do you hope to get out of this study, and why?

Close this segment by spending a few moments asking God to honor the desires shared in response to question 3.

●

With the time that remains, review the following considerations, working your way around the group's circle with members reading the points aloud in round-robin style. Then enjoy some unhurried conversation—perhaps over snacks!

- *Prayer.* We learn in Mark 11:24 that when we ask God for anything that is in accordance with his will, we will receive it. Prioritize prayer both now and throughout the coming eight weeks. Ask God to round off rough edges of selfishness, pride, distraction, and fear that keep us from committing ourselves to the cause of unity in our world.

- *Consistency.* Please prioritize each of the coming eight sessions and mark them on your calendar. Everyone is busy, but everyone's participation *matters.* Help maintain our group's continuity and intimacy, which will grow cumulatively week on week, by deciding to show up each time we're scheduled to meet . . . and then, in fact, showing up.

- *Engagement.* Just as you will show up bodily, plan to show up emotionally and spiritually too. Plan to engage actively in each discussion, candidly and thoughtfully sharing your input as you're invited to do so.

- *Openness.* As much as possible, as you engage in the group discussion each week, work to keep an open mind and an open heart. Work to maintain a nonjudgmental atmosphere where members can freely share their thoughts, questions, and experiences. This concept cuts right to the heart of what being *life-minded* truly means—resolving to set aside differences for the purpose of prizing unity, both within the church and beyond.

- *Confidentiality.* You will notice as you work through these sessions that the level of expected candor increases each week. Please hold fast to the rule of confidentiality: *whatever is shared in our group stays in our group.*

- *Thoroughness.* While your discretionary time each week will vary, try as much as possible to complete the Solo Study segments (four per week) prior to showing up to the following week's group time. Our weekly discussion will also be deepened if you read the chapter in *Life-Minded: 8 Practices for Belonging to God and Each Other* that corresponds to each session's spiritual practice.

- *Preparedness.* Be sure to review the commitment you made at the end of the previous session so you can report back to your group on how things went.

To prepare for next week's session on devotion, please read chapter 4 of *Life-Minded: 8 Practices for Belonging to God and Each Other.*

Session 01

Devotion

Session Setup

What does it mean to practice *devotion*? The official definition, according to Merriam-Webster, is this: "religious fervor: piety; an act of prayer or private worship; . . . the act of dedicating something to a cause, enterprise, or activity; . . . the fact or state of being ardently dedicated and loyal."[1]

In Christian circles we might say it this way: *devotion is steadfast commitment to an object of worship.*

As human beings, we were created to live lives of devotion. We were crafted to be worshipers at heart. We were meant to connect, to attach, to invest ourselves, to join with others. None of that is in question. Rather, the question is to what or whom we will devote ourselves. *This* is what we must decide.

To follow God is to adhere to the instructions laid out in the Word of God, the Bible. And to understand God's Word is to see that our devotion is to be reserved for God—and God alone. "Ascribe to the LORD the glory due his name," writes David in 1 Chronicles 16:29. "Bring an offering and come before him. Worship the LORD in the splendor of his holiness."

"All the earth bows down to you," the psalmist writes in Psalm 66:4. "They sing praise to you, they sing the praises of your name."

"Yet a time is coming and has now come when the true worshipers will worship the Father in the Spirit and in truth, for they are the kind of worshipers the Father seeks," says Jesus in John 4:23.

"Worship the Lord your God and serve him only," Jesus says in Luke 4:8.

We are to glorify God.

We are to bow down to God.

We are to praise God.

We are to serve God.

We aren't just to be worshipers. We are to exclusively worship God.

We aren't merely to be devoted. We're to live devoted to God alone.

As believers, we long to live this way, even as distraction tempts us at every turn.

Is this kind of steady and fullhearted devotion to God even possible? we wonder. *Is the gap between how I wish to live and how I actually live one that can ever be closed?*

In this session, we'll explore not only those questions but these as well:

- Why are we supposed to live solely devoted to God?
- How do we cultivate full devotion to God?
- How can we know if we are practicing full devotion to God?
- What can we expect from a fully devoted life lived for Christ?

Let's dig in!

Opener

Before you screen this session's video, share your thoughts on the following questions.

Considering your current season of life and the specific circumstances you're facing, would you say that your days feel more *filled* or *fulfilled* lately?

What rhythms, habits, priorities, or observations are fueling your assessment of your days?

THE JESUS ENCOUNTER: Mark 1:21–39

The following Bible passage will be read aloud during the video. The text appears here for your reference.

They went to Capernaum, and when the Sabbath came, Jesus went into the synagogue and began to teach. The people were amazed at his teaching, because he taught them as one who had authority, not as the teachers of the law. Just then a man in their synagogue who was possessed by an impure spirit cried out, "What do you want with us, Jesus of Nazareth? Have you come to destroy us? I know who you are—the Holy One of God!"

"Be quiet!" said Jesus sternly. "Come out of him!" The impure spirit shook the man violently and came out of him with a shriek.

The people were all so amazed that they asked each other, "What is this? A new teaching—and with authority! He even gives orders to impure spirits and they obey him." News about him spread quickly over the whole region of Galilee.

As soon as they left the synagogue, they went with James and John to the home of Simon and Andrew. Simon's mother-in-law was in bed with a fever, and they immediately told Jesus about her. So he went to her, took her hand and helped her up. The fever left her and she began to wait on them.

That evening after sunset the people brought to Jesus all the sick and demon-possessed. The whole town gathered at the door, and Jesus healed many who had various diseases. He also drove out many demons, but he would not let the demons speak because they knew who he was.

Very early in the morning, while it was still dark, Jesus got up, left the house and went off to a solitary place, where he prayed. Simon and his companions went to look for him, and when they found him, they exclaimed: "Everyone is looking for you!"

Jesus replied, "Let us go somewhere else—to the nearby villages—so I can preach there also. That is why I have come." So he traveled throughout Galilee, preaching in their synagogues and driving out demons.

 Video Notes

As you watch the video, log impactful phrases or key takeaways based on the prompts below.

Worship, connect, serve

When we live in full devotion to God

Scriptures that champion godly devotion

When good intentions aren't enough

Jesus had to pray

Cut flowers and rooted trees

The necessity of God's Word

Where can you always be found?

Only what the Father has taught us

Group Discussion

Work through the following questions in full group, addressing as many as time and interest permit.

1. What was the most meaningful quote or concept from the video for you, and why?

2. When you think about what you're devoted to during this season of life, what comes to mind?

3. In the video I said, "I think you'd agree that after his radical conversion on the road to Damascus, the apostle Paul lived a fully devoted life. In his letter to the Colossian church, he wrote, 'Whatever you do, whether in word or deed, do it all in the name of the Lord Jesus, giving thanks to God the Father through him' [Colossians 3:17]. And so we want to live this way—*every* word, *every* deed, doing *all that we do* in the name of Jesus Christ." Do you agree that true believers long to be devoted to God? How would you describe your desires in this regard?

4. What do the following Bible verses tell you about why God demands your exclusive allegiance?

Scripture Verse(s)	Insight Discovered
Exodus 20:3–6	
Romans 12:1–2	
Philippians 3:7–11	
Revelation 4:11	

5. Three categories of distraction tend to derail our efforts to live fully devoted to God. Which of the three hit closest to home for you, and why?

   ▪ *Your devices*: any form of technological escapism—scrolling social media for hours on end, binge-watching a favorite show, "chain listening" to podcasts or audiobooks so that you're rendered unavailable to others for large chunks of time

   ▪ *Your "drug" of choice*: the nightly glass (or two) of wine you can't do without, the tendency to overeat nonnutritious foods, the coffee addiction that leaves you perpetually wired and tired

   ▪ *Your day planner*: the insistence that you can plan your way out of every bind . . . that with a little more organization, a touch more control, a few more lists, you can become the person you hope to be

6. While the Bible is clear that we cannot earn salvation, it's also clear that once we become believers, God expects us to steward the divine power living inside of us (his Spirit) in noble ways. These are the "works" we read about in verses such as James 2:26: "Just as the body is dead without breath, so also faith is dead without good works" (NLT).

   Consider the list below of good works we're intended to pursue. How might living *fully devoted to God* help you achieve these objectives more regularly, more effortlessly, and even more joyfully? Select one from the list that you'd like to share your thoughts on.

- pleasing God (Colossians 1:10)
- cultivating a habit of prayer (1 Thessalonians 5:16–18)
- reading God's Word faithfully and applying its instruction (Psalm 1:2–3)
- maintaining a heart for the lost (Romans 10:11–15)
- sharing the gospel with people who don't know God (Matthew 28:19–20)
- being known for our love (John 13:35)
- practicing always the fruit of the Spirit—love, joy, peace, patience, kindness, goodness, faithfulness, gentleness, and self-control (Galatians 5:22–23 NLT)
- practicing temperance and being careful not to uphold habits that cause others to stumble (1 Corinthians 8:9)
- being good listeners and attending to others' needs with empathy and ready action (Romans 12:15; James 1:19)
- respecting authority (Hebrews 13:17)
- being both truthful and loving in our speech (Ephesians 4:15)
- persevering amid difficult circumstances (2 Corinthians 4:16–18)
- being hospitable, extending relational warmth to all (1 Peter 4:9)

7. God promises that when we live lives of full devotion to him, we will receive access to an abundance of supernatural resources that help us face whatever circumstances and challenges come our way, including the following:

   ■ strength (Psalm 28:7)

   ■ provision (Matthew 6:33)

   ■ protection (Psalm 121:7–8)

   ■ wisdom (Proverbs 2:6)

   ■ peace (Isaiah 26:3)

   Which of these resources do you most desire today? Why?

8. If we faithfully uphold this first practice—that of *living fully devoted to God*—then the other practices in this study will take care of themselves. If true—and the Scriptures themselves say it is!—then living fully devoted to God will set in motion other laudable practices in our lives:

   • Our full devotion to God will catalyze *curiosity* regarding others' circumstances and needs.

   • Our full devotion to God will catalyze *discernment* regarding how we might help meet those needs.

   • Our full devotion to God will catalyze a posture not of antagonism toward the world but of *peace*.

   • Our full devotion to God will catalyze a spirit not of selfishness but of *service*.

   • Our full devotion to God will catalyze *forgiveness* toward those who have wronged us, recognizing that Christ himself was also terribly wronged.

- Our full devotion to God will catalyze *awe* toward God and his creation.

- Our full devotion to God will catalyze both our willingness and our ability to extend *grace* to those who need it most.

How does this reality of devotion to God catalyzing these other practices make you feel?

Praying It Through

In pairs, consider before God your answers to the following questions, asking God to encourage you in your quest to live more fully devoted to him.

1. Think about your walk with Christ thus far. When have you been most devoted to him and to the spiritual practices that help you walk more closely with him day by day?

2. How are you spending your time lately? What do you always make time for? What things that you say are important to you somehow never seem to make it into your day?

3. Which relationships, attachments, involvements, habits, or—
   gulp—devices would be most difficult for you to give up, and
   why?

As you pray, ask God to help you see the state of your heart clearly.
Pray the words of Psalm 26:2: "Test me, LORD, and try me, exam-
ine my heart and my mind."

Thank him for seeing you and for caring about you. Thank him
for telling you the truth about the things that are holding you back
from unencumbered intimacy with him. Thank him for being committed to closing the gap between who you are today and the person you long to be.

The Challenge

*Before ending today's session, share which of the commitments
below you plan to uphold this week.*

To prioritize devotion to God, this week I will . . .

- Keep my phone in a different room than where I sleep and
  give myself the gift of at least one tech-free hour in the morning before looking at my phone.
- Log my prayers—as in, literally write them out.
- Pause during idle moments, and instead of reaching for my
  favorite distraction ask God, "Where are you at work in my
  life, Father? What do you want me to know? What do you
  want me to see? What do you want me to do?"
- Take a complete break from social media.

- _____

_____

Note any thoughts or plans in the space below.

If I were to make the plainest case to you for devoting yourself to Jesus more than you devote yourself to your phone, it would be this: only one of those resources holds all wisdom, encouragement, and understanding in his hands, and that resource undeniably is God. Whatever is troubling you about the world today, *God absolutely longs to redeem it*. He has perspective. He has insight. He has counsel. He has grace. And he longs to pass all those things to you.

—*Life-Minded*

Solo Study: Day 1 of 4

Devoted in Heart

Date Completed: _____

This week, we will meditate on the four aspects of how Jesus defined full devotion to God and ask God to shore up our commitment in these specific areas of life. You might want to refer back to Praying It Through from group study time.

Read: Mark 12:28–30 NLT

One of the teachers of religious law was standing there listening to the debate. He realized that Jesus had answered well, so he asked, "Of all the commandments, which is the most important?"

Jesus replied, "The most important commandment is this: 'Listen, O Israel! The LORD our God is the one and only LORD. And you must love the LORD your God with all your heart, all your soul, all your mind, and all your strength.'"

Reflect

Consider the following questions based on the first part of Jesus's injunction, which is to love God with all your heart.

1. What do I love with all my heart?

2. Which of these objects of my heartfelt affection bring me closer to God? Which seem to take me further from him—from his will, his ways, his wishes for me?

3. Scripture indicates that I, as a follower of Jesus, will love things such as the Word of God and the people in the world, as well as things such as mercy and goodness and kindness. How loving am I feeling toward these things lately?

Receive

The Bible tells us that when we practice godly love, ordering our affections according to his will and ways, we will realize many divine benefits, including the following:

- We will know a love that is of God (1 John 4:7–8).
- We will know a love that cannot coexist with fear (1 John 4:18).
- We will know a love that cannot fail (1 Corinthians 13:8).

Which of these promises is most meaningful to you today, and why?

Solo Study: Day 2 of 4

Devoted in Soul

Date Completed: _____

Read: Mark 12:28–30 NLT

One of the teachers of religious law was standing there listening to the debate. He realized that Jesus had answered well, so he asked, "Of all the commandments, which is the most important?"

Jesus replied, "The most important commandment is this: 'Listen, O Israel! The LORD our God is the one and only LORD. And you must love the LORD your God with all your heart, all your soul, all your mind, and all your strength.'"

Reflect

Consider the following questions based on the second part of Jesus's injunction, which is to love God with all your soul.

1. Why is it important to devote my soul—the eternal part of me—to God?

2. Have I surrendered my soul to the lordship of Christ?

3. What does it mean in my everyday life to live surrendered to Christ?

Receive

The Bible tells us that when we surrender our souls to God through faith in his Son, Jesus Christ, we are afforded many benefits, including the following:

- forgiveness of sins (1 John 1:9)
- eternal life with God (John 3:16)
- guidance during life on earth (Proverbs 3:5–6)
- strength for whatever circumstances we face (Philippians 4:13)
- joy (John 16:24)

Which of these promises is most meaningful to you today, and why?

Solo Study: Day 3 of 4

Devoted in Mind

Date Completed: _____

Read: Mark 12:28–30 NLT

One of the teachers of religious law was standing there listening to the debate. He realized that Jesus had answered well, so he asked, "Of all the commandments, which is the most important?"

Jesus replied, "The most important commandment is this: 'Listen, O Israel! The LORD our God is the one and only LORD. And you must love the LORD your God with all your heart, all your soul, all your mind, and all your strength.'"

Reflect

Consider the following questions based on the third part of Jesus's injunction, which is to love God with all your mind.

1. What kind of thoughts do I tend to entertain most often?

2. Do my typical thoughts draw me into God's presence or repel me from it?

3. How often do I think about all that God has done for me, about all that I'm grateful for?

Receive

In 1 Corinthians 14:15, the apostle Paul reminds believers at Corinth that they can pray not only in the Spirit but also with the mind. He writes, "I will pray with my spirit, but I will pray with my mind also; I will sing praise with my spirit, but I will sing with my mind also" (ESV).

What might it look like for you to focus today on *singing to God with your mind*, with your thoughts?

Solo Study: Day 4 of 4

Devoted in Strength

Date Completed: _____

Read: Mark 12:28–30 NLT

One of the teachers of religious law was standing there listening to the debate. He realized that Jesus had answered well, so he asked, "Of all the commandments, which is the most important?"

Jesus replied, "The most important commandment is this: 'Listen, O Israel! The LORD our God is the one and only LORD. And you must love the LORD your God with all your heart, all your soul, all your mind, and all your strength.'"

Reflect

Consider the following questions based on the fourth and final part of Jesus's injunction, which is to love God with all your strength.

1. What am I naturally good at?

2. How often do I engage these natural giftings specifically for the glory of God?

3. What might it mean to use my gifts, talents, and abilities as conduits for deeper devotion to God?

Receive

In 1 Corinthians 12:12–28, Paul explains that as believers we are all part of one body. He writes:

> The human body has many parts, but the many parts make up one whole body. So it is with the body of Christ. Some of us are Jews, some are Gentiles, some are slaves, and some are free. But we have all been baptized into one body by one Spirit, and we all share the same Spirit.
>
> Yes, the body has many different parts, not just one part. If the foot says, "I am not a part of the body because I am not a hand," that does not make it any less a part of the body. And if the ear says, "I am not part of the body because I am not an eye," would that make it any less a part of the body? If the whole body were an eye, how would you hear? Or if your whole body were an ear, how would you smell anything? . . .
>
> All of you together are Christ's body, and each of you is a part of it. Here are some of the parts God has appointed for the church:
>
> first are apostles,
> second are prophets,
> third are teachers,
> then those who do miracles,

those who have the gift of healing,
those who can help others,
those who have the gift of leadership,
those who speak in unknown languages.
(vv. 12–17, 27–28 NLT)

How might you deepen your understanding of your spiritual gifts, which your natural talents and abilities point to? Consider taking the following steps:

- Pray. Ask God which gift(s) he has given you.
- Journal. Spend a few minutes logging your thoughts about your gifting.
- Practice. As you engage with others today, be intentional about using your gift(s) and talents for the glory of God. For example, if someone compliments how organized you always are, instead of receiving the affirmation for yourself, say, "I praise God for that! I wasn't always this way, but he has helped me become a more well-ordered person."

To prepare for next week's session on curiosity, please read chapter 5 of *Life-Minded: 8 Practices for Belonging to God and Each Other*.

SESSION 01 INSIGHTS + IDEAS

Curiosity

Session Setup

In our fast-paced world, where information is ridiculously readily available, the virtue of curiosity is often overshadowed by the need for quick answers and immediate gratification. It's unfortunate, really, because curiosity is what fosters engagement and meaningful connections with other people, and it's a practice endorsed by the apostle Paul in Philippians 2:4. There we read that we are to "look not only to [our] own interests, but also to the interests of others" (ESV). Further, King Solomon reminds us in Proverbs 20:5 that "the purposes of a person's heart are deep waters, but one who has insight draws them out." We can't draw out another's deep-seated ways without curiosity.

The overshadowing of curiosity is also unfortunate because making a habit of being curious beautifully aligns with biblical principles that encourage things like empathy, compassion, and grace. Having a posture of curiosity in conversation involves the willingness to inquire about others' thoughts, feelings, and experiences, caring *about* people as a precursor to perhaps caring *for* them.

When you practice curiosity in conversation, you signal your active interest in the other person, which can make him or her feel seen, heard, and valued.

When you practice curiosity in conversation, you promote your own learning and understanding.

When you practice curiosity in conversation, you forge a connection with the other person that self-absorption can never achieve.

Embracing curiosity in conversation not only enriches our understanding of others and the world but also deepens our spiritual growth by fostering a genuine quest for knowledge and truth. And to be lovers of Jesus is to be utterly captivated with what is true.

Opener

Before you screen this session's video, share your thoughts on the following questions.

What was the last situation or conversation where someone genuinely took an interest in your perspective or point of view?

How did it make you feel, and what impact did it have on the interaction?

THE JESUS ENCOUNTER: Matthew 16:13–17

The following Bible passage will be read aloud during the video. The text appears here for your reference.

When Jesus came to the region of Caesarea Philippi, he asked his disciples, "Who do people say the Son of Man is?"

They replied, "Some say John the Baptist; others say Elijah; and still others, Jeremiah or one of the prophets."

"But what about you?" he asked. "Who do you say I am?"

Simon Peter answered, "You are the Messiah, the Son of the living God."

Jesus replied, "Blessed are you, Simon son of Jonah, for this was not revealed to you by flesh and blood, but by my Father in heaven."

 Video Notes

As you watch the video, log impactful phrases or key takeaways based on the prompts below.

"Come, Holy Spirit"

What your day holds . . . and whom

Ask, and ask again

The greatest question asker

People matter

The gifts of curiosity

Who people are

Where people are

What has motivated significant shifts

Start with hello

Group Discussion

Work through the following questions in full group, addressing as many as time and interest permit.

  1. What stood out to you during this session's video, and why?

2. Why do you suppose it's so common for human beings to prejudge others instead of approaching them in a spirit of curiosity so they can get to know them for who they truly are?

3. In the chapter on curiosity in *Life-Minded*, I wrote of a time when a fellow resident of my city assumed I held certain views because of my position as a middle-aged, white, male megachurch pastor.

    Perhaps you can relate. Think of a time when someone prejudged you, drawing conclusions about you that were untrue. How did you feel? What residual effects, if any, existed for you hours, days, or even years later?

4. Turning the tables for a moment (ugh!), when have you prejudged another person, only to discover later that *your* assessment was incorrect?

    Consider the list of common ways we tend to prejudge others on page 40 to see if any memories come to mind. Collect your thoughts; then, if you're comfortable doing so, share an abbreviated version of the experience with your group.

Appearance	Communication Style	Interpersonal Preference
Making assumptions about people based on clothing, hairstyle, or other superficial choices they have made	Assuming that people who speak with a certain accent or use certain verbiage are a specific type of person	Assuming things about people based on their apparent introversion or extroversion
Economic Standing	**Age**	**Gender**
Making assumptions about people because of your perception of their financial station	Assuming that people should or shouldn't, or can or can't, do something because of their season in life	Assuming that people ought to hold certain preferences or behave in a certain way because of their gender
Social Connections	**Interests and Hobbies**	**Lifestyle Decisions**
Assuming that people affiliated with that person or group must then be like this	Assuming that because someone likes a certain activity, she or he must believe certain things or behave in a certain way	Making assumptions about people based on preferences regarding nutrition, exercise, time management, politics, etc.

In our present outrage culture, I can't be the only one who is struggling both with the aggravation of being pre-judged and with the wild temptation to prejudge others. It's a terrible plight, really, being caught from both sides in this way.

—*Life-Minded*

5. In Matthew 16:15, Jesus asked Simon Peter, "Who do you say I am?" Why do you think Jesus asked Simon Peter this question if Jesus, being all-knowing, already knew the answer?

6. Take a look below at the list of laudable characteristics of people who practice curiosity in conversation. Which ones do you most often demonstrate in your interactions with others? Which ones would you most benefit from now, and why?

   Spend a few minutes jotting down helpful notes or memories in the spaces below each quality before sharing your thoughts with your group.

   ■ *Open-Mindedness*: the willingness to hear diverging perspectives and to ask follow-up questions to better understand those views

   ■ *Empathy*: the ability to put yourself in others' shoes and consider things from their vantage point

   ■ *Generosity*: the graciousness to invest unhurried time and unselfish energy in interpersonal interactions so that conversations can expand and breathe

■ *Connectivity*: the desire to relate with people beyond a superficial level and the determination to build deep, meaningful relationships with those you know

■ *Patience*: the forbearance to allow others to share their thoughts and opinions freely, fully, and at their own pace

7. Consider the self-reflective questions below. Based on these facets of curiosity, would you say you are a curious person? What practices, habits, or tendencies shape your perception of yourself in this regard?

■ Do I enjoy learning new things?
■ Am I typically inquisitive in conversation?
■ Am I always asking "why" and "how" questions?
■ Do I enjoy solving problems . . . even if they're not my own?
■ Am I open to (and even inquisitive about) people's perspectives that differ from my own?
■ Do I explore new hobbies or interests from time to time?
■ Am I drawn to books or other sources of new information?
■ Do I enjoy discovering things I don't already know?
■ Am I comfortable with uncertainty?
■ Do people sometimes seem honored by the sincere questions I ask them?

If you wanted to further improve your "curiosity quotient," which of these ideas might you begin practicing? Exploring a new hobby? Being more intentionally inquisitive in conversation? Learning something new? Capture your answer below.

Praying It Through

In pairs, consider before God your answers to the following questions, asking God to encourage you in your quest to engage others with a spirit of curiosity.

1. If you're honest with yourself, would you say you've been more concerned lately with managing your own circumstances or with understanding the circumstances others are walking through?

2. What fears, insecurities, attitudes, circumstances, or plain old habits might be keeping you from taking a genuine interest in other people's lives more often than you currently do?

3. What supernatural resources does God promise you in Scripture that might empower you to authentically engage with others instead of spending all your energy on your own concerns? (The Solo Study days from session 1 on pages 25–33 list many divine resources if you need ideas.)

As you pray, ask God to reinforce in your mind and heart the apostle Paul's exhortation in Romans 12:9–10: "Love from the center of who you are; don't fake it. Run for dear life from evil; hold on for dear life to good. Be good friends who love deeply; practice playing second fiddle" (MSG).

Thank him for equipping you to love others well by taking a genuine interest in their lives.

The Challenge

Before ending today's session, discuss in full group how last week's challenge went, and then share which of the commitments below you plan to uphold this week.

To prioritize the practice of curiosity, this week I will . . .

- Begin each day by asking God to prepare me for the interactions I know I'll have and to help me ask thoughtful questions.
- Pay close attention to assumptions or prejudgments I am tempted to make of others and as often as possible squelch them before they get translated into words.
- Memorize Philippians 2:3–4 (the anchor text for this session's four Solo Study segments) and ask God to help me embody its message.

■ Seek counsel from a good question asker in my life regarding how I might demonstrate authentic curiosity more often in my conversations.

■ _____

_____

Note any thoughts or plans in the space below.

Curious people are universally seen as warmer, kinder, and more physically attractive than their counterparts. Ask a question, why don't you! You'll get better looking every time.

—*Life-Minded*

Solo Study: Day 1 of 4
Rejecting Self-Centeredness

Date Completed: _____

This week, we will meditate on four aspects of taking a genuine interest in others, according to the apostle Paul's words to the believers at Philippi found in Philippians 2:3–4.

Read: Philippians 2:3–4

Do nothing out of selfish ambition or vain conceit. Rather, in humility value others above yourselves, not looking to your own interests but each of you to the interests of the others.

Reflect

Consider the following questions based on the first part of the apostle Paul's injunction to believers to take a genuine interest in others by avoiding selfishness.

1. Most days, would I say I spend my best time and energy focused on my own needs and concerns or on the needs and concerns of others? What attitudes, assumptions, or circumstances influence my focus here?

2. How unselfish do I think it is prudent to be, and why?

3. What do I make of the example of selflessness demonstrated in Jesus's life throughout the Gospels?

Receive

Look up Proverbs 11:25 and write out the verse below.

When have you experienced the truth of this verse firsthand? What were the circumstances, and what happened as a result?

What insights did you gather that could serve you well when you are next tempted to make things all about you?

Solo Study: Day 2 of 4
Humbling Yourself

Date Completed: _____

Read: Philippians 2:3–4

Do nothing out of selfish ambition or vain conceit. Rather, in humility value others above yourselves, not looking to your own interests but each of you to the interests of the others.

Reflect

Consider the following questions based on the second part of the apostle Paul's injunction to believers to take a genuine interest in others by practicing humility.

1. What does it mean to humble myself?

2. Why does Paul assert that believers need humility to value others above self?

3. What might the by-products be if I were to prioritize the practice of humbling myself?

Receive

What assurance do you find in Psalm 147:6 regarding those who practice humility?

What do you think it means to be sustained by God?

Based on the circumstances you are facing today, what do you *hope* it means?

Solo Study: Day 3 of 4

Valuing Others

Date Completed: _____

Read: Philippians 2:3–4

Do nothing out of selfish ambition or vain conceit. Rather, in humility value others above yourselves, not looking to your own interests but each of you to the interests of the others.

Reflect

Consider the following questions based on the third part of the apostle Paul's injunction to believers to take a genuine interest in others by valuing others.

1. How do I hope people will see me as I make my way through the world?

2. What unspoken rules do I hold regarding who is worthy of my attention and care?

3. What habits or patterns would I need to adjust to start valuing *everyone* as priceless creations of God?

Receive

In John 3:16, we see how devoted God is to the crown of his creation: people . . . *all* people. There, we read: "For God so loved the world that he gave his one and only Son, that whoever believes in him shall now perish but have eternal life."

Why is this act of devotion important to you?

How does God's radical act of devotion inspire you to regard, consider, or value the people you encounter in daily life?

Solo Study: Day 4 of 4

Prioritizing Others

Date Completed: _____

Read: Philippians 2:3–4

Do nothing out of selfish ambition or vain conceit. Rather, in humility value others above yourselves, not looking to your own interests but each of you to the interests of the others.

Reflect

Consider the following questions based on the fourth and final part of the apostle Paul's injunction to believers to take a genuine interest in others by prioritizing others' interests and concerns.

1. Who are a few people I know well? (These could be nuclear or extended family members, friends, neighbors, or close work associates.) What is concerning them these days? What interests are they juggling just now?

Name/Relation	Primary Concerns/Needs

2. What role does *curiosity* play in making the previous exercise a straightforward—even easy—one?

3. What do I suppose is meant in this week's key Bible passage when Paul exhorts believers to value others by "looking to" their interests?

What might it mean for me to *look to* the interests of the people I noted in the grid above?

Receive

Luke 6:38 carries a promise regarding living with generosity of spirit toward others. Look up the verse and write it out below.

What would you say is the "measure" you use in prioritizing the needs and concerns of those in your life?

What would you *like* your measure to be, and why?

To prepare for next week's session on discernment, please read chapter 6 of *Life-Minded: 8 Practices for Belonging to God and Each Other.*

SESSION 02 INSIGHTS + IDEAS

Discernment

Session Setup

In the previous session, we looked at the power of curiosity for developing muscles of compassion and empathy toward those we come across. Indeed, taking a genuine interest in someone else by asking a question—and then a follow-up question (or three!) after that—is always the first step in forging a relational connection.

The reason *that* session preceded *this* session is because this session centers on using our words wisely once the conversation naturally shifts to the topic of us. And we don't need to worry about that until we've placed the spotlight on the other person first. We do well to operate according to the words of Proverbs 18:13 in this regard: "To answer before listening—that is folly and shame." When we rush to speak without fully comprehending the nuances of a situation or another person's viewpoint, we risk contributing to division rather than dispelling it.

In this session, we'll look at Jesus's example of using his words to glorify his Father and ponder what it might mean to pattern our speech after his. We'll commit ourselves to speaking only words that *comfort* the other person, words that *confirm* something God has said to the other person or wishes to say through us, and words that joyfully *cooperate* with God's activity in the world. "Do not let any unwholesome talk come out of your mouths," the apostle Paul wrote to the believers at Ephesus in Ephesians 4:29, "but only what is helpful for building others up according to their needs, that it may benefit those who listen."

Admittedly, this is a weighty burden we bear—stewarding our speech in helpful and edifying ways—but God promises to divinely equip us to live in the way he has asked us to live. By embracing these practices of listening well to others before we contribute to the dialogue with great discernment, we can contribute to the healing and reconciliation of a divided world. We can build bridges, extend grace, and exemplify the teachings of Christ, who himself listened intently and spoke words of profound wisdom and love.

Opener

Before you screen this session's video, share your thoughts on the following questions.

In the chapter on discernment in *Life-Minded*, I recount a time when I stood in line at the airport behind a guy who was giving the desk agent a tough time. In recent days, when have you encountered someone similarly shrouded in the "spirit of jerk"? (Hopefully it wasn't you!) What were the circumstances, and why were the person's words so unhelpful?

THE JESUS ENCOUNTER: John 7:37–52

During this session's Group Discussion, a group member will be asked to read the following Bible passage aloud.

On the last and greatest day of the festival, Jesus stood and said in a loud voice, "Let anyone who is thirsty come to me and drink. Whoever believes in me, as Scripture has said, rivers of living water will flow from within them." By this he meant the Spirit, whom those who believed in him were later to receive. Up to that time the Spirit had not been given, since Jesus had not yet been glorified.

On hearing his words, some of the people said, "Surely this man is the Prophet."

Others said, "He is the Messiah."

Still others asked, "How can the Messiah come from Galilee? Does not Scripture say that the Messiah will come from David's descendants and from Bethlehem, the town where David lived?" Thus the people were divided because of Jesus. Some wanted to seize him, but no one laid a hand on him.

Finally the temple guards went back to the chief priests and the Pharisees, who asked them, "Why didn't you bring him in?"

"No one ever spoke the way this man does," the guards replied.

"You mean he has deceived you also?" the Pharisees retorted. "Have any of the rulers or of the Pharisees believed in him? No! But this mob that knows nothing of the law—there is a curse on them."

Nicodemus, who had gone to Jesus earlier and who was one of their own number, asked, "Does our law condemn a man without first hearing him to find out what he has been doing?"

They replied, "Are you from Galilee, too? Look into it, and you will find that a prophet does not come out of Galilee."

 ### Video Notes

As you watch the video, log impactful phrases or key takeaways based on the prompts below.

Two ears, one mouth

Weapon to harm, tool to heal

Good communicators practice

God is wise, and he shares

Jesus's "strange" speech

What ought to be true of us

Prophecy 101

Words of comfort

Words of confirmation

Words of cooperation

Group Discussion

Work through the following questions in full group, addressing as many as time and interest permit.

1. Would those who know you best say you're a more enthusiastic *listener* or a more enthusiastic *speaker*? Would you agree with their assessment? Why or why not?

2. What makes a good listener? When have you felt deeply listened to by another?

3. What makes a good speaker or conversationalist? Who in your relational sphere do you consider to be an exceptional communicator? Why?

———————————— ● ————————————

I've often said that where two or three are gathered together, an argument is bound to ensue. . . . We *want* to be agreeable; it's just that in most cases if we choose to agree with the other person, then we'd both be wrong. Am I right?

—Life-Minded

4. How often do you feel stymied in conversation because you don't know what to say or how to articulate what you are thinking or feeling? Select the answer that best reflects your experience, and then explain your answer to your group.

   ▦ "All. The. Time. *So* frustrating."
   ▦ "Frequently. I wish I were better at using my words well."
   ▦ "Sometimes. Especially if I'm tired or distracted."
   ▦ "Rarely. I'm pretty good shooting from the hip conversationally."
   ▦ "Almost never. I read both rooms and people well and consistently voice apt words."

5. The Bible is full of counsel on how to speak well no matter the situation. What do the following verses teach regarding stewarding our words wisely? Look up one verse, note the takeaway, and then share it with the group.

Verse(s)	Counsel on Using Words Well
Proverbs 15:28	
Ephesians 4:29	
James 1:19	
Proverbs 15:4	
Colossians 4:6	
Matthew 12:36–37	

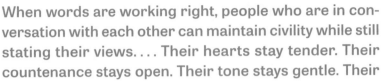

When words are working right, people who are in conversation with each other can maintain civility while still
stating their views.... Their hearts stay tender. Their
countenance stays open. Their tone stays gentle. Their
laughter comes easy and quick.

—*Life-Minded*

6. A key aspect to stewarding our words wisely is understanding
how to cultivate a "prophetic imagination." What comes to
mind when you hear the term *prophecy*?

What assumptions, beliefs, or firsthand experiences shape
your perception of what prophecy is all about?

7. How does the definition of prophecy in the video, which centers on using words to "comfort, confirm, and cooperate"
with God in the work he's accomplishing in and through people's lives, reflect the takeaways from Scripture you noted on
the grid in question 5?

8. Read aloud for the group the Jesus Encounter from John
7:37–52, found on pages 57–58 above, regarding Jesus's
"strange" speech. How open would you say you are to having

God transform your speech, so that going forward you only use your words to comfort others, confirm his activity, and cooperate with his agenda in other people's lives?

What fears or insecurities spring to mind as you consider such a reality in your life?

Praying It Through

In pairs, consider before God your answers to the following questions, asking God to encourage you in your quest to use your words wisely day by day.

1. Do you believe that God could use your words to comfort others, to confirm his work in their midst, and to cooperate with his work in and through their lives?

2. Do you believe that God will place such words on your tongue on a just-in-time basis? Do you trust him to do so?

3. Can you envision a version of yourself that is marked by wise speech? What do you suppose God has in store for you in that more deeply transformed state?

As you pray, ask God to refine your desires such that you long to be *righteous* in conversation with others more than you long to be witty or charming or right.

Thank him for the promise in Philippians 1:6, where the apostle Paul reminded believers at Philippi that God would continue transforming them until the day that Jesus returned. The same promise exists for us. God will never stop refining us, renewing us, shaping us in the image of his Son, Jesus Christ.

The Challenge

Before ending today's session, discuss in full group how last week's challenge went, and then share which of the commitments below you plan to uphold this week.

To prioritize discernment, this week I will . . .

- ▪ Fall silent when I'm tempted to say something discouraging, disparaging, or negative.
- ▪ Ask God to give me the courage to comfort another person with my words when I would normally stay silent for fear of overstepping a relational boundary.
- ▪ Pray each morning for opportunities to use my words well.
- ▪ Make a habit of asking God, *What are you up to in this person's life?* when I'm in the middle of a conversation with someone else . . . and then, if appropriate, telling the other person what God conveys to me.

■ Refrain from criticizing another person this week, even if the criticism is warranted! (Remember that this commitment is for the purpose of refining your heart, not the other person's behavior.)

■ _____

_____

Note any thoughts or plans in the space below.

Solo Study: Day 1 of 4

Avoid What Is Unwholesome

Date Completed: _____

This week, we will meditate on four highly practical ways to use our words wisely that come straight from the pages of Scripture.

Read: Ephesians 4:29

Do not let any unwholesome talk come out of your mouths, but only what is helpful for building others up according to their needs, that it may benefit those who listen.

Reflect

Consider the following questions based on the first part of Paul's exhortation in Ephesians 4:29 to use our words wisely by avoiding unwholesome talk.

1. When have I been the subject of another person's unkind speech? How did it feel? What might those feelings teach me about the usefulness of measuring my own speech?

2. When I cave to speaking words that are gossipy or detrimental to others, what am I seeking? Attention? Affection? Inclusion? Something else?

3. What does it mean to me to seek God's glory in the way I use my words instead of seeking attention, affection, or inclusion from the world?

Receive

Tomorrow, when you look back on the words you spoke today, what adjectives will you hope to be true of them? Add your own words to the list started below.

- wise
- kind
- measured
- true

If you strung together two days, two weeks, two months, two years, or two decades of using your words in this manner, what do you suppose would be the impact in the exchanges and relationships God places you in?

Solo Study: Day 2 of 4
Speak What Is Helpful

Date Completed: _____

Read: Ephesians 4:29

Do not let any unwholesome talk come out of your mouths, but only what is helpful for building others up according to their needs, that it may benefit those who listen.

Reflect

Consider the following question based on the second part of Paul's exhortation in Ephesians 4:29 to use our words wisely by speaking only what is helpful.

> What are three helpful things I've said this week that I can praise God for—three times when by his mercy and power I used my words to uplift and encourage another person?

1.

2.

3.

Receive

The book of Proverbs tells us that when we practice discernment in our speech, we can

- bring about healing in our relationships (12:18; 16:24);
- offer inspiration to others (10:11); and
- provide guidance to those navigating life's tough circumstances (20:5).

Which of these promises do you long for today? Why?

Solo Study: Day 3 of 4

Adapt to the Need

Date Completed: _____

Read: Ephesians 4:29

Do not let any unwholesome talk come out of your mouths, but only what is helpful for building others up according to their needs, that it may benefit those who listen.

Reflect

Consider the following questions based on the third part of Paul's exhortation in Ephesians 4:29 to use our words wisely by adapting to others' needs.

1. How often do I think—*really* think—about others as I engage in conversation with them?

2. What would it look like for me to adapt to others' circumstances throughout the next twenty-four hours as I talk with them?

   ■ I could say, "I'd love to be a listening ear for you if you'd like to say more."

   ■ I could say, "Would you mind backing up this story a little? I'm embarrassed to admit that my thoughts were elsewhere, and I really want to focus on what you're telling me."

■ I could say, "I'm so sorry to have to run right now, but let me ask you this: May I text you tonight to set up a call for later this week? I want to have an unrushed conversation with you soon." ·

■ _____

_____

Receive

Think about a time when a listener in your life adapted his or her conversation to perfectly suit your needs. What are a few aspects of that memory that you can thank God for now? In the space below, form your thoughts into a prayer of thanksgiving to God.

Solo Study: Day 4 of 4

Benefit All

Date Completed: _____

Read: Ephesians 4:29

Do not let any unwholesome talk come out of your mouths, but only what is helpful for building others up according to their needs, that it may benefit those who listen.

Reflect

Consider the following questions based on the fourth and final part of Paul's exhortation in Ephesians 4:29 to use our words wisely to benefit those who listen.

1. What does it mean to benefit someone I'm talking with?

2. After I talk with others, do I get the sense that they are *more encouraged and uplifted* or *less encouraged and perhaps a little overwhelmed* because they conversed with me? What does my answer reflect about my level of relational and conversational discernment?

3. What can I learn from Psalm 19:14 regarding the connection between surrendering my heart more fully to God's leadership and being able to more regularly use my words wisely?

Receive

In Proverbs 18:21 Solomon wrote that "the tongue has the power of life and death, and those who love it will eat its fruit."

Considering a difficult situation you see unfolding today, either in the world at large or in your specific corner of it, what words or phrases could you utter to wield each of these powers?

Words and phrases that would likely contribute to death:

•

•

•

•

•

Words and phrases that would likely contribute to life:

•

•

•

•

•

To prepare for next week's session on peace, please read chapter 7 of *Life-Minded: 8 Practices for Belonging to God and Each Other.*

SESSION 03 INSIGHTS + IDEAS

Session 04

Peace

Session Setup

Peace. The word alone accomplishes its meaning. *Peace.* Say it aloud and feel your heart rate and mental spin cycle slow.

Think of the occasion, recorded in three of the Gospels, when Jesus was on a boat with his disciples as a violent storm erupted. As the story goes, seeing the whipping wind and sky-high waves, the disciples caved to distress and fear. Would they get out of this thing alive?

Simultaneously, Jesus was sound asleep. Not distressed. Not afraid.

Fearing for their lives, the disciples woke him, likely with sweat on their brows and grave concern on their faces. "Lord, save us!" they cried, according to Matthew's account. "We're going to drown!" (8:25).

Jesus, unfazed by the drama of his men, woke up. He stood up. And then he said to the wind and waves, "Peace!" (Mark 4:39 ESV).

The text describes his command as a rebuke, and evidently the storm (wisely) complied, falling immediately into a state of calm. It was an authoritative display of Jesus's supernatural power. It was also a profound teaching moment for his disciples as they realized that when peace was needed, peace was what Jesus would provide. When turmoil descended, when fear had a stranglehold, when circumstances spiraled out of control, there rested Jesus, completely unfazed, prepared to usher in peace.

He remains our source of peace today.

Whenever we sense that we've shifted from relative calm to outright chaos, we can turn to Jesus in our distress and fear and ask him to come to our aid. In a world marked by division, following Jesus's example of de-escalation is a powerful way to be a beacon of peace. We can extend empathy instead of judgment. We can build bridges instead of blowing them up. We can be a life-minded voice of reason instead of ramping up the tension. We can push for peace in an ever-increasingly divisive world.

Opener

Before you screen this session's video, share your thoughts on the following questions.

Describe a time when you were deeply—and perhaps in hindsight comically—infuriated over a set of circumstances that were beyond your control.

What was the situation? Why were you so revved up? How did things get resolved?

● THE JESUS ENCOUNTER: Mark 3:1–6

During this session's Group Discussion, a group member will be asked to read the following Bible passage aloud.

Another time Jesus went into the synagogue, and a man with a shriveled hand was there. Some of them were looking for a reason to accuse Jesus, so they watched him closely to see if he would heal him on the Sabbath. Jesus said to the man with the shriveled hand, "Stand up in front of everyone."

Then Jesus asked them, "Which is lawful on the Sabbath: to do good or to do evil, to save life or to kill?" But they remained silent.

He looked around at them in anger and, deeply distressed at their stubborn hearts, said to the man, "Stretch out your hand." He stretched it out, and his hand was completely restored. Then the Pharisees went out and began to plot with the Herodians how they might kill Jesus.

 Video Notes

As you watch the video, log impactful phrases or key takeaways based on the prompts below.

What peaceful people know

The reason for Jesus's gift

A key skill to cultivate

Held by the bond of peace

Step one in peacemaking

The journalist's deep breath

What to cancel instead of people

Take our feelings to God

The response of compassion

The demand for dignity

Group Discussion

Work through the following questions in full group, addressing as many as time and interest permit.

1. How have you been impacted by "cancel culture," which began to take root with the widespread adoption of social media? What do you think is the motivation behind the ever-increasing trend of people condemning those who disagree with them to the point of trying to erase them from the once-free exchange of ideas?

2. Describe a time when you had trouble accessing peace recently. What was the situation, and why did peace feel elusive?

   What are your thoughts on the "bond of peace" as described in the video? Why do you think Paul made a direct connection between unity and peace in Ephesians 4:3?

3. Do you agree that assuming "people are doing the best they can with the information that they have" is a good way to move through the world in a less reactive manner? Why or why not?

Holding space often means creating a place of engagement, understanding, and transformative growth.

—Life-Minded

4. After a group member has read aloud the passage in "The Jesus Encounter" on pages 77–78 above, answer the following questions.

Several themes rise to the surface in this account of Jesus healing a man with a withered hand on a Sabbath. Which ones noted below seem most applicable to you, given the issues you see plaguing our world today? Why? Any you'd add to the list?

- *Choosing compassion over legalism.* Jesus made a point of asking the religious leaders if they thought it was more important to help a man in need or to uphold the rigid regulations concerning the Sabbath.

- *Choosing activity over passivity.* Jesus could have expressed concern for the man verbally—or even nonverbally—without going to the effort of activating that concern.

- *Choosing integrity over hypocrisy.* Jesus challenged the religious elite by showing them that while they were so busy trying to catch Jesus breaking the Sabbath laws, they were allowing a man right in front of them to suffer.

- *Choosing calmness over conflict.* Jesus neither ignored the Pharisees' misbehavior nor escalated the conflict that their behavior provoked. Instead, he defended his decision to heal the man and then withdrew.

- _____

  _____

5. What practices help you come to your daily interactions as a person of peace? How often would you say you've experienced this sturdy peacefulness during your present season of life?

6. We've talked so far in this study about the practices of being fully devoted to God, approaching people from a posture of curiosity, and using discerning words to edify and empower people in their walk with God. How do you suppose each of these practices helps you be an agent of unity in your corner of the world? Complete one of the prompts below, and then share with your group.

The connection I see between my level of devotion to God and my ability to be a unifying force in my world is . . .

I think curiosity fosters unity by . . .

I can see discerning words being a powerful tool for bringing unity to a conversation or situation by . . .

Praying It Through

In pairs, consider before God your answers to the following questions, asking God to encourage you in your quest to live as a person of peace in an increasingly vitriolic world.

1. Are you quicker in conversation to notice differences between you and other people or to discern common ground?

2. Whenever a conversation you're part of grows tense, do you usually feel compelled to "say your piece," or are you more apt to withdraw? Something in between?

3. What thoughts, feelings, or emotions rise in you as you consider Jesus's example of bringing peace instead of strife both to interactions during his earthly ministry and to the world at large by willingly facing death on a cross?

As you pray, ask God to *envision* you for being a person of peace in increasingly meaningful ways. Ask him to help you seek harmony and understanding in conversations with other people, even if that means you aren't able to defend your position or persuade others of your beliefs. Trust that as God wants you to tell others about him, his promptings will be obvious to you and the exchanges will flow smoothly, respectfully, and in a manner marked by compassion.

Thank him for the gift of his divine peace, which the apostle Paul says "transcends all understanding" and "will guard your hearts and your minds in Christ Jesus" (Philippians 4:7).

The Challenge

Before ending today's session, discuss in full group how last week's challenge went, and then share which of the commitments below you plan to uphold this week.

To honor God by prioritizing peacemaking, this week I will . . .

- Calmly communicate a boundary in a relationship where strife exists. (You might say, "I really respect your passion for your beliefs, but I wonder if we might talk about something less contentious with the few minutes we have together.")

- Actively empathize with people I find myself in conversation with by placing myself in their shoes, by remembering that they are created in the image of God, by considering that they may be doing the best they can do today. (Instead of casting judgment on them, you might ask about their journey in coming to a specific perspective or about what motivated them to pursue a particular course of action.)

- Become a warrior for the cause of *being patient* with others. (You might allow a few beats of silence in a conversation instead of jumping in with your ideas and perspectives.)

- Refuse to push people's buttons by avoiding topics I know cause division between others and me.

- Think through two or three respectful, even *unifying*, topics I'll be ready to introduce with friends and perfect strangers alike. (You might come to an exchange having prepared your thoughts on an inspiring book you read or on a good-news story you caught in your feeds. Or you might come prepared to ask another person about what she or he has been reading, learning, or doing to enjoy the current season.)

- _____

_____

Note any thoughts or plans in the space below.

If we will take God at his word that he is good, and he is holy, and he is the very definition of faithful to us, if we will "do away with the yoke of oppression, with the pointing finger and malicious talk," as Isaiah 58:9 says, then our "light will rise in the darkness" and our "night will become like the noonday" (v. 10).

—*Life-Minded*

Solo Study: Day 1 of 4

Embrace Peace as a Blessing

Date Completed: _____

This week, we will meditate on four aspects of practicing peace-making in our daily lives.

Read: Matthew 5:9 AMP

Blessed [spiritually calm with life-joy in God's favor] are the makers *and* maintainers of peace, for they will [express His character and] be called the sons of God.

Reflect

Consider the following questions based on the first part of Jesus's injunction in Matthew 5:9 to live as makers and maintainers of the gift of peace by embracing peace as a blessing.

1. Where does peacemaking fit into my understanding of a blessed life—a life that aligns with the way of Jesus?

   Where does peacemaking fit into my *current practice* of living as a reflection of Jesus in the world?

Where do I long for peacemaking to fit? In other words, how intentional do I *wish I were* about becoming a person unwaveringly committed to promoting and preserving peace?

2. Which posture most threatens my willingness or ability to focus more intently on becoming an active peacemaker in my world?

- "My point of view on _____ is right, and I'm not interested in hearing contrary views."
- "My perspective on what it means to be a believer in this day and age means I can't engage with people who disagree with me."
- "My preferred inputs—news sources, online media outlets, and friend groups—confirm that I just can't budge on the critical topics of our day."
- "I can't handle exposing myself to all the disunity in the world today. My heart can't take the amount of vitriol I see and hear."
- "Honestly, I wouldn't even know where to start in trying to bring peace to such a divisive environment."
- "My choosing to be a person of peace won't make even a hint of difference in a world that seems only to prize exclusion, hatred, and strife."

- _____

_____

Receive

In Psalm 1:1–3, the psalmist likens the Godward life to being a tree planted by streams of water:

> Blessed is the one
> > who does not walk in step with the wicked
> or stand in the way that sinners take
> > or sit in the company of mockers,
> but whose delight is in the law of the LORD,
> > and who meditates on his law day and night.
> That person is like a tree planted by streams of
> > water,
> > which yields its fruit in season
> and whose leaf does not wither—
> > whatever they do prospers.

Assuming that peacemaking is a critical aspect of Godward living, which benefit of peacemaking do you most long to realize during this season of your life?

- ☐ avoiding divisive discussions and behaviors
- ☐ delighting in God's principles
- ☐ sitting with and being moved by God's Word in fresh ways
- ☐ actively promoting reconciliation and harmony in my corner of the world
- ☐ contributing to the well-being of the communities I am a part of

Solo Study: Day 2 of 4
Actively Pursue Peace

Date Completed: _____

Read: Matthew 5:9 AMP

Blessed [spiritually calm with life-joy in God's favor] are the makers *and* maintainers of peace, for they will [express His character and] be called the sons of God.

Reflect

Consider the following questions based on the second part of Jesus's injunction in Matthew 5:9 to live as makers and maintainers of the gift of peace by actively pursuing peace.

1. In which of my current relationships am I experiencing significant strife?

2. As I sit with that situation before me, what am I sensing that God would have me do to be a peacemaker in that relationship?

3. What fears or insecurities have kept me from pursuing those actions thus far?

4. What step—even if it's just a baby step—am I willing to take today to lay aside my fears and frustrations to pursue peace in this relationship?

Receive

In John 14:27, Jesus said to his disciples, "My peace I give you."

Based on this promise, how might you choose to be impacted today in your own sense of inner peace and in your determination to find peace in challenging circumstances?

Solo Study: Day 3 of 4
Reflect God's Character

Date Completed: _____

Read: Matthew 5:9 AMP

Blessed [spiritually calm with life-joy in God's favor] are the makers *and* maintainers of peace, for they will [express His character and] be called the sons of God.

Reflect

Consider the following questions based on the third part of Jesus's injunction in Matthew 5:9 to live as makers and maintainers of the gift of peace by expressing God's character.

1. How would those who know me best describe my character? What observable habits would they point to in order to justify their perception of me?

2. What do I make of the Amplified Bible version of Matthew 5:9 drawing a direct correlation between peacemaking as a practice and reflecting God's character as an expression?

Receive

Read Genesis 1:27–28.

> So God created mankind in his own image,
>   in the image of God he created them;
>   male and female he created them.
>
> God blessed them and said to them, "Be fruitful
> and increase in number; fill the earth and subdue
> it. Rule over the fish in the sea and the birds in the
> sky and over every living creature that moves on the
> ground."

What was God's first action after creating humankind in his image?
What does this tell you about the heart of God toward the crown of
his creation, his children?

Solo Study: Day 4 of 4

Recognize Your Identity in Christ

Date Completed: _____

Read: Matthew 5:9 AMP

Blessed [spiritually calm with life-joy in God's favor] are the makers *and* maintainers of peace, for they will [express His character and] be called the sons of God.

Reflect

Consider the following questions based on the fourth and final part of Jesus's injunction in Matthew 5:9 to live as makers and maintainers of the gift of peace by recognizing our identity as children of God.

1. When I think about my identity, what words, phrases, or descriptors come to mind?

2. Did "child of God" make my list in response to question 1? Why or why not?

3. What does it mean to be a *child of God*?

Receive

In Matthew 5:9, Jesus tells us that when we practice peacemaking, we will be called children of God. This promise carries with it several implications:

- Children of God have a family, a support structure, as they move through the world and face the challenges inherent in this life.
- Children of God have a loving heavenly Father who is eager to see them, to communicate with them, to protect them, and to provide for their needs.
- Children of God are image bearers of the Creator of the universe, God himself. As such, they carry with them inherent worth, power, creativity, goodness, and beauty.

Which of these promises is most meaningful to you today? Why?

To prepare for next week's session on service, please read chapter 8 of *Life-Minded: 8 Practices for Belonging to God and Each Other*.

SESSION 04 INSIGHTS + IDEAS

Service

Session Setup

It's wonderful to take an interest in people by asking good questions, by engaging in meaningful conversation, even by praying earnestly over their needs. But doing these wonderful things apart from *acting* on that well-placed concern is settling for a watered-down form of what it means to follow Christ. To align our lives with the example Jesus set during his earthly ministry is to *couple works* with our wonderful faith.

Consider what the apostle James (and half brother of Jesus) wrote in James 2:14–19:

> What good is it, my brothers and sisters, if someone claims to have faith but has no deeds? Can such faith save them? Suppose a brother or a sister is without clothes and daily food. If one of you says to them, "Go in peace; keep warm and well fed," but does nothing about their physical needs, what good is it? In the same way, faith by itself, if it is not accompanied by action, is dead.
>
> But someone will say, "You have faith; I have deeds."
>
> Show me your faith without deeds, and I will show you my faith by my deeds. You believe that there is one God. Good! Even the demons believe that—and shudder.

James wrote these words to a broad audience of Jewish communities that had been scattered and were living in various locations instead of as a unified group. But their applicability is just as strong for us here and now, more than two thousand years later, as it was for them then. *All* believers need James's reminder not to merely believe Jesus's teachings but also to demonstrate those beliefs through regular, tangible action.

In this session we'll look at both how to rightly reframe the obligations that usurp much of our daily lives and how to respond quickly and joyfully to divine appointments our heavenly Father sets for us.

Opener

Before you screen this session's video, share your thoughts on the following questions.

What words or phrases come to mind when you hear the term *servant*?

What experiences or assumptions do you think have shaped your perception?

THE JESUS ENCOUNTER: John 6:1–15

The following Bible passage will be read aloud during the video. The text appears here for your reference.

Some time after this, Jesus crossed to the far shore of the Sea of Galilee (that is, the Sea of Tiberias), and a great crowd of people followed him because they saw the signs he had performed by healing the sick. Then Jesus went up on a mountainside and sat down with his disciples. The Jewish Passover Festival was near.

When Jesus looked up and saw a great crowd coming toward him, he said to Philip, "Where shall we buy bread for these people to eat?" He asked this only to test him, for he already had in mind what he was going to do.

Philip answered him, "It would take more than half a year's wages to buy enough bread for each one to have a bite!"

Another of his disciples, Andrew, Simon Peter's brother, spoke up, "Here is a boy with five small barley loaves and two small fish, but how far will they go among so many?"

Jesus said, "Have the people sit down." There was plenty of grass in that place, and they sat down (about five thousand men were there). Jesus then took the loaves, gave thanks, and distributed to those who were seated as much as they wanted. He did the same with the fish.

When they had all had enough to eat, he said to his disciples, "Gather the pieces that are left over. Let nothing be wasted." So they gathered them and filled twelve baskets with the pieces of the five barley loaves left over by those who had eaten.

After the people saw the sign Jesus performed, they began to say, "Surely this is the Prophet who is to come into the world." Jesus, knowing that they intended to come and make him king by force, withdrew again to a mountain by himself.

Video Notes

As you watch the video, log impactful phrases or key takeaways based on the prompts below.

The weird thing about vocational ministry

Not role but relationship

The beauty of divine appointments

Seeing those in need

To puff up or to lie low

The tired and hungry crowd

What God longs for us

A dangerous prayer

Eyes that see

Group Discussion

Work through the following questions in full group, addressing as many as time and interest permit.

1. What are some of the opportunities for service you feel obligated to act on during this present season of your life?

2. How would you describe your posture toward the "mandatory" acts of service you mentioned in response to question 1?

Are you pleased or displeased with your posture? Why?

3. Whenever Jesus approached a crowd of people with deep needs, he saw them as "sheep without a shepherd" (Matthew 9:36). What do you take from Jesus's assessment? How do you think such an assessment prompted him to act on the crowd's behalf?

4. If a spirit of humility is a precursor to being used by God to serve others, why don't more believers joyfully pursue the things that will yield humility in their lives?

5. What types of pursuits tend to yield humility in the life of a Christ follower? Working in full group, build a bulleted list below. (If you need ideas, revisit John 6:1–15, being attentive to the thoughts, attitudes, words, actions, and decisions of Jesus himself as he saw many people in need.)

-
-
-
-
-
-
-
-

When we cooperate with God's redemptive activity in the world, we reflect the passion and purpose of Jesus, who "did not come to be served, but to serve, and to give his life as a ransom for many" (Mark 10:45). For the believer, there is no higher aim in life than to *become* like the one we serve.

—Life-Minded

6. In *Life-Minded*, I make the statement, "Our spiritual senses are never sharper than when we are walking humbly with our God." When have you found this to be true your own life? What were the circumstances that "brought you low," and what shift in your spiritual senses did you detect?

Praying It Through

In pairs, consider before God your answers to the following questions, asking God to encourage you in your quest to live a life of enthusiastic service in his name.

1. How concerned are you about others' well-being? What attitudes, actions, or inactions would you point to in support of your self-assessment in this regard?

2. How effectively are you balancing obligated service with responding to divine appointments during the season you're in?

3. In your heart of hearts, are you more *grateful* or *resentful* whenever you encounter an opportunity to serve? What do you think about your posture toward service these days?

————————————————— ◗ —————————————————

When we genuinely choose to take the high road by going low—by letting go of our sense of entitlement, by laying down our preferences and demands, by caring more about others being elevated than about securing the win for ourselves—it is then that God will raise us up.

—Life-Minded

As you pray, ask God to give you vivid clarity to see the opportunities to serve that he'd have you seize. Ask him to transform you into a servant who is more joyful than ever to reflect his love in the world by helping to meet others' needs.

Thank him for his promise that he is trustworthy to promote you at just the right time, and that you can opt for humility instead of fighting to promote yourself.

The Challenge

Before ending today's session, discuss in full group how last week's challenge went, and then share which of the commitments below you plan to uphold this week.

To prioritize a heart of service, this week I will . . .

- ▪ Pray daily for a spirit of humility.
- ▪ Choose to view my acts of "mandatory" service as gifts, not burdens.
- ▪ Seek out an opportunity to serve someone in need who cannot repay the gesture.
- ▪ Memorize and meditate on the words of Mark 10:45 (from the key passage for this session's Solo Study).
- ▪ Ask someone at my church how I can begin volunteering there.

■ Join a group I've been thinking of aligning with and pursue serving opportunities there.

■ _____

_____

Note any thoughts or plans in the space below.

Solo Study: Day 1 of 4

Reject the World's Way

Date Completed: _____

This week, we will meditate on four aspects of cultivating a heart of service, based on the words of Jesus in Mark 10:42–45.

Read: Mark 10:42–45

Jesus called them together and said, "You know that those who are regarded as rulers of the Gentiles lord it over them, and their high officials exercise authority over them. Not so with you. Instead, whoever wants to become great among you must be your servant, and whoever wants to be first must be slave of all. For even the Son of Man did not come to be served, but to serve, and to give his life as a ransom for many."

Reflect

Consider the following questions based on the first part of Mark's account of what Jesus said about cultivating a heart of service by rejecting the world's idea of authority.

1. Jesus begins his remarks by contrasting the way the world uses power to abuse people instead of serve them. When have you seen power used for improper purposes? What was the effect on those who were subjected to it?

2. Jesus was the most powerful person ever to walk the planet. Why do you think he opted for servant leadership instead of adopting the world's way?

Receive

In Proverbs 16:17–19, King Solomon reminds us of the benefits of going low in a spirit of humility, even as the rest of the world goes high in a spirit of pride.

> The highway of the upright avoids evil;
> those who guard their ways preserve their lives.
>
> Pride goes before destruction,
> a haughty spirit before a fall.
>
> Better to be lowly in spirit along with the
> oppressed
> than to share plunder with the proud.

Meditate for a few moments on what it means to have your life preserved as you choose to walk in humility along the path of righteousness God has paved for you. Which aspect of having your life preserved is most meaningful to you today, and why?

Solo Study: Day 2 of 4
Embrace Servanthood

Date Completed: _____

Read: Mark 10:42–45

Jesus called them together and said, "You know that those who are regarded as rulers of the Gentiles lord it over them, and their high officials exercise authority over them. Not so with you. Instead, whoever wants to become great among you must be your servant, and whoever wants to be first must be slave of all. For even the Son of Man did not come to be served, but to serve, and to give his life as a ransom for many."

Reflect

Consider the following questions based on the second part of Mark's account of what Jesus said about cultivating a heart of service by embracing servanthood.

1. Do I think Jesus is being literal when he says that to be great I must be a servant, that "whoever wants to be first must be slave to all"? Why or why not?

2. How often do I willingly—even enthusiastically—step to the back of the line, so to speak, instead of more assertively satisfying my needs or desires?

3. Would I rather be known for the greatness that comes from earthly success or the greatness that comes from servanthood? Why?

Receive

As you consider adopting Jesus's approach to greatness, allow the words of Saint Augustine to encourage you today: "Do you wish to rise? Begin by descending. You plan a tower that will pierce the clouds? Lay first the foundation of humility."[2]

What might it look like for you to add one more brick to the foundation of humility in your life today?

Solo Study: Day 3 of 4

Respond to the Call

Date Completed: _____

Read: Mark 10:42–45

Jesus called them together and said, "You know that those who are regarded as rulers of the Gentiles lord it over them, and their high officials exercise authority over them. Not so with you. Instead, whoever wants to become great among you must be your servant, and whoever wants to be first must be slave of all. For even the Son of Man did not come to be served, but to serve, and to give his life as a ransom for many."

Reflect

Consider the following questions based on the third part of Mark's account of what Jesus said about cultivating a heart of service by answering his call.

1. As a believer in Jesus, have I ever considered myself called to service? Do I see Jesus's words in Mark 10:42–45 as such a call? Why or why not?

2. Jesus seems to imply that inherent in humankind is the push for greatness, the desire to be at the head of the line. When have I sensed this dynamic in my own thoughts and desires? Do I think Jesus is saying here that this natural push is evil?

3. How often would I say that God can rely on me to seize an opportunity to serve that he has called me to?

Receive

The apostle Paul reminds the Corinthian church in one of his letters that when we choose to devote ourselves to serving others as God directs, we can be sure that we've chosen well. "Therefore, my dear brothers and sisters, stand firm. Let nothing move you. Always give yourselves fully to the work of the Lord, because you know that your labor in the Lord is not in vain" (1 Corinthians 15:58).

What does it mean to you today that investing yourself in the work of the Lord is investing in something that is worthwhile, not just in our present reality but for all eternity?

Be fair in your dealings. Be compassionate toward people. Take God more seriously than you take yourself. See how life works out when you do. See if God doesn't readily use you to help fix something that's broken in your world.

—*Life-Minded*

Solo Study: Day 4 of 4

Follow Christ's Example

Date Completed: _____

Read: Mark 10:42–45

Jesus called them together and said, "You know that those who are regarded as rulers of the Gentiles lord it over them, and their high officials exercise authority over them. Not so with you. Instead, whoever wants to become great among you must be your servant, and whoever wants to be first must be slave of all. For even the Son of Man did not come to be served, but to serve, and to give his life as a ransom for many."

Reflect

Consider the following questions based on the fourth and final part of Mark's account of what Jesus said about cultivating a heart of service by following his lead.

1. As God incarnate, Jesus rightly could have requested—even demanded—to be served during his time on earth. Why didn't he?

2. When have I found it helpful in my daily life that Jesus set a clear example of how I am to serve?

3. Why does God choose to work through me as his follower in serving the needs of people in the world when he could accomplish his purposes directly?

Receive

The Scriptures are full of good news for those who pattern their lives after the example of Jesus Christ. Read through the list below, ticking the ones that resonate most with you today.

- *Salvation and eternal life.* In John 14:6, Jesus says, "I am the way and the truth and the life. No one comes to the Father except through me." This is the *ultimate* good news, that on surrendering by faith to the lordship of Jesus Christ, you will receive salvation and eternity with God.
- *Purpose and meaning.* Closing his exhortation to his disciples that they not worry about the practical concerns of life, Jesus said this: "But seek first his kingdom and his righteousness, and all these things will be given to you as well" (Matthew 6:33).
- *Spiritual transformation.* The apostle Paul writes in 2 Corinthians 3:18, "And we all, who with unveiled faces contemplate the Lord's glory, are being transformed into his image with ever-increasing glory, which comes from the Lord, who is the Spirit."
- *Fruitfulness.* In John 15:5, Jesus promises, "I am the vine; you are the branches. If you remain in me and I in you, you will bear much fruit; apart from me you can do nothing."

- *Peace and rest.* Jesus says in Matthew 11:28, "Come to me, all you who are weary and burdened, and I will give you rest."

- *Divine favor and blessings.* Jesus makes this promise in the Sermon on the Mount: "Blessed are those who hunger and thirst for righteousness, for they will be filled" (Matthew 5:6).

- *Eternal rewards.* "Rejoice and be glad," Jesus says in Matthew 5:12, speaking of those who suffer for the sake of righteousness, "because great is your reward in heaven."

To prepare for next week's session on forgiveness, please read chapter 9 of *Life-Minded: 8 Practices for Belonging to God and Each Other.*

SESSION 05 INSIGHTS + IDEAS

Forgiveness

Session Setup

In this session we'll look at the profound and deeply transformative concept of *forgiveness*. Forgiveness isn't always easy, especially when the person who has wronged us isn't sorry or hasn't asked for forgiveness. But the Bible teaches us that the practice of forgiveness is meant to be a fundamental aspect of our faith journey.

One of the best-known passages on forgiveness can be found in the Lord's Prayer, where Jesus teaches us to pray, "Forgive us our debts, as we also have forgiven our debtors" (Matthew 6:12). He goes on to say, "For if you forgive other people when they sin against you, your heavenly Father will also forgive you. But if you do not forgive others their sins, your Father will not forgive your sins" (vv. 14–15). In other words, forgiveness doesn't just benefit the person being forgiven; it also benefits the one who chooses to forgive.

Together we'll look at three truths regarding forgiveness, the first being that *forgiveness is a liberating act*. When we choose to forgive, we release the grip that another's actions have on us and thus free ourselves from the bondage of resentment, anger, and bitterness. In Colossians 3:13, we are urged to "bear with each other and forgive one another if any of you has a grievance against someone. Forgive as the Lord forgave you." This verse highlights that our forgiveness is modeled after God's forgiveness of our own sins. The freedom we know when we forgive stems from the freedom God first offered to us.

Second, *forgiveness is an ongoing act.* It's a daily choice to let go of the hurt, to relinquish the desire for revenge, and to extend grace to those who have wronged us. In Luke 17:3–4, Jesus advises, "If your brother or sister sins against you, rebuke them; and if they repent, forgive them. Even if they sin against you seven times in a day and seven times come back to you saying 'I repent,' you must forgive them." This passage reminds us that forgiveness knows no limits but rather is a continuous act of mercy.

Third, *forgiveness is an act of love.* In 1 Corinthians 13:5, love "keeps no record of wrongs." When we love as Christ loved us, we are compelled to forgive, regardless of whether the other person expresses remorse.

We may face no greater challenge in daily life than to wholly and earnestly forgive others for their wrongdoing. But equally true, we may know no greater satisfaction than when we are released from the burden of bitterness to reflect the grace and love we have received from God.

Opener

Before you screen this session's video, share your thoughts on the following questions.

Without naming names, what type of person do you have trouble forgiving? Why?

⬤ THE JESUS ENCOUNTER: Luke 23:26–49

The following Bible passage will be read aloud during the video. The text appears here for your reference.

As the soldiers led him away, they seized Simon from Cyrene, who was on his way in from the country, and put the cross on him and made him carry it behind Jesus. A large number of people followed him, including women who mourned and wailed for him. Jesus turned and said to them, "Daughters of Jerusalem, do not weep for me; weep for yourselves and for your children. For the time will come when you will say, 'Blessed are the childless women, the wombs that never bore and the breasts that never nursed!' Then

> "'they will say to the mountains, "Fall on us!"
> and to the hills, "Cover us!"'

For if people do these things when the tree is green, what will happen when it is dry?"

Two other men, both criminals, were also led out with him to be executed. When they came to the place called the Skull, they crucified him there, along with the criminals—one on his right, the other on his left. Jesus said, "Father, forgive them, for they do not know what they are doing." And they divided up his clothes by casting lots.

The people stood watching, and the rulers even sneered at him. They said, "He saved others; let him save himself if he is God's Messiah, the Chosen One."

The soldiers also came up and mocked him. They offered him wine vinegar and said, "If you are the king of the Jews, save yourself."

There was a written notice above him, which read: THIS IS THE KING OF THE JEWS.

One of the criminals who hung there hurled insults at him: "Aren't you the Messiah? Save yourself and us!"

But the other criminal rebuked him. "Don't you fear God," he said, "since you are under the same sentence? We are punished justly, for we are getting what our deeds deserve. But this man has done nothing wrong."

Then he said, "Jesus, remember me when you come into your kingdom."

Jesus answered him, "Truly I tell you, today you will be with me in paradise."

It was now about noon, and darkness came over the whole land until three in the afternoon, for the sun stopped shining. And the curtain of the temple was torn in two. Jesus called out with a loud voice, "Father, into your hands I commit my spirit." When he had said this, he breathed his last.

The centurion, seeing what had happened, praised God and said, "Surely this was a righteous man." When all the people who had gathered to witness this sight saw what took place, they beat their breasts and went away. But all those who knew him, including the women who had followed him from Galilee, stood at a distance, watching these things.

 Video Notes

As you watch the video, log impactful phrases or key takeaways based on the prompts below.

Family baggage times ten

Who is it for you?

Who Jesus struggled to forgive

Lessons from Luke 23

What to forgive

When to forgive

Why to forgive

What to harbor instead of resentment

Radical forgiveness

Group Discussion

Work through the following questions in full group, addressing as many as time and interest permit.

1. How would you describe your posture regarding the subject of forgiveness? Which previous experiences or current perspectives shape that posture?

2. Describe a time when someone earnestly forgave you. Without necessarily divulging the details of what needed to be forgiven, put words to how being forgiven made you feel. How did the relationship change from there?

3. What offense would you say is *beyond* forgiveness, if any? Has anyone ever committed this offense against you?

If I were to name the central challenge facing us as believers in our day, it's that instead of seeing people as image
bearers of God whom we're called to see and serve and
love, we've come to see them as the distraction, the enemy,
the cause of our dis-ease and distress. When I was a kid,
the national pastime was baseball; today, I'd say it's disgrace. We disgrace anyone and everyone who has an
opinion that is different from ours. We disparage them,
we dehumanize them, and, figuratively at least, we kick
them to the curb.

—*Life-Minded*

4. Have you ever forgiven someone who didn't ask for forgiveness? What motivated you to do so?

5. Revisit Luke 23:26–49. Working quickly in full group, complete the following grid, writing down both the offenses Jesus
faced and his responses. Note that there isn't always a one-to-
one correlation between the two.

Offense(s) against Jesus	Jesus's Response

6. Jesus accessed a wealth of divine resources to maintain his posture of radical forgiveness. Which do you wish you tapped into more often, and why?

- *Unconditional love.* Jesus demonstrated what John 3:16 says to be true: "For God so loved the world that he gave his one and only Son." His unconditional love enabled him to love those who were being cruel to him.

- *Divine purpose.* Jesus was clear on his purpose while on earth, which was to provide salvation for humanity by testifying to the truth (John 18:37; 1 Timothy 1:15). This sense of purpose empowered him to prevail against opposition and stay focused on the end game.

- *Full surrender to God's will.* Jesus said in Luke 22:42, "Father, if you are willing, take this cup from me; yet not my will, but yours be done." His submission allowed him to forgive, even when it meant enduring great suffering.

- *Compassion and empathy.* Jesus understood the spiritual blindness of those who were harming him. He knew they were "sheep without a shepherd" (Mark 6:34), which moved him to extend forgiveness to them.

- *Spiritual authority.* Jesus easily could have called upon divine intervention or judgment to get him out of his predicament, but instead he chose forgiveness, emphasizing his divine authority over sin and death.

- *A vision of future redemption.* Jesus knew his sacrifice would open the door to forgiveness and reconciliation between God and humanity. This perspective allowed him to forgive in the face of suffering.

- *Faith in God's justice.* Jesus trusted that by leaving vengeance in his Father's hands (see Romans 12:19), God, who alone judges the hearts and actions of all individuals, would one day make all things right.

7. What did you make of the assertion that instead of harboring resentment, we as believers are called to "harbor love"?

Praying It Through

In pairs, consider before God your answers to the following questions, asking God to encourage you in your quest to practice quick and thorough forgiveness.

1. How do you feel about the wrongs that have been done to you? What obstacles to true and complete forgiveness rise to the surface of your heart?

2. How committed are you to practicing forgiveness, no matter how deep the hurt, no matter how persistent the pain?

3. How would life be different if you laid down every last ounce of resentment, trusting that as you pass the weight to God, he will make all things right in due time?

As you pray, ask God to fortify your heart so you can offer forgiveness without hesitation or the expectation of getting anything in return.

Thank him for going before you to show you through the example of Jesus how to forgive fully and swiftly, holding nothing back, holding no grudges, holding nothing but love in your heart for the people he came to save.

The Challenge

Before ending today's session, discuss in full group how last week's challenge went, and then share which of the commitments below you plan to uphold this week.

To prioritize the practice of forgiveness, this week I will . . .

- Reflect on and journal about my own need for forgiveness—both ultimately, which Jesus extended to me upon my salvation, and on an ongoing basis as I occasionally misstep my way through life.

- Pray through a psalm for each person I need to forgive. (Consider Psalms 20; 23; 67; 91; and 121.)

- Practice the "pause and pray" method. As I find myself triggered by people or situations, I will take a moment to ask God for guidance and then respond with a forgiving heart.

- Meditate on and memorize Colossians 3:12–14, which exhorts believers to forgive and connects the principles of forgiveness and love.

- Write a letter of forgiveness. I will put my words of forgiveness down on paper as a way to process my thoughts and feelings, even if I never plan to send the letter.

- Seek reconciliation. If appropriate and safe, I will approach a person I need to forgive with the intent of seeking reconciliation. Jesus encouraged this action in Matthew 5:23–24 when he said, "Therefore, if you are offering your gift at the altar and there remember that your brother or sister has something against you, leave your gift there in front of the altar. First go and be reconciled to them; then come and offer your gift."

▧ Let go of a grudge. I will make a conscious effort to release a grudge I've been carrying far too long, remembering that holding on to those negative feelings only harms me in the long run.

▧ _____

_____

Note any thoughts or plans in the space below.

As believers, we are called not to push people away from God's kingdom but to *envision* them for inhabiting it eternally by the ways that we love and lead. And in my estimation, there is no more effective or efficient way to do this than to practice forgiveness toward others and to receive God's forgiveness for ourselves.

—*Life-Minded*

Solo Study: Day 1 of 4

What Fuels Forgiveness

Date Completed: _____

This week, we will meditate on four aspects of practicing forgiveness by focusing on the apostle Paul's words from Colossians 3:12–14.

Read: Colossians 3:12–14

Therefore, as God's chosen people, holy and dearly loved, clothe yourselves with compassion, kindness, humility, gentleness and patience. Bear with each other and forgive one another if any of you has a grievance against someone. Forgive as the Lord forgave you. And over all these virtues put on love, which binds them all together in perfect unity.

Reflect

Consider the following questions based on the first part of Paul's exhortation to pursue forgiveness by clothing ourselves in Christlikeness.

1. In what ways do I see the character traits of compassion, kindness, gentleness, and patience fueling a spirit of forgiveness?

2. If I were to grow in one of these traits to help deepen my practice of quick and thorough forgiveness, which would I focus on first? Why?

■ compassion   ■ gentleness
■ kindness   ■ patience

3. What is one tangible step I can take to begin focusing on this trait?

Receive

The Bible tells us that when we practice clothing ourselves in righteousness—putting on what Paul calls the "fruit of the Spirit" in Galatians 5:22–23—we receive many divine gifts. Sit with the following list, allowing your soul to be refreshed as you ponder the goodness God has planned for you, as you entrust your days to him.

- Spiritual growth
- Spiritual fulfillment
- Practical fulfillment
- Joy
- Harmony in relationships
- Inner peace
- Positive influence
- Favor with God and with others
- Spiritual strength
- Spiritual resilience
- Impact in the world
- Eternal rewards

Solo Study: Day 2 of 4

What Forgiveness Entails

Date Completed: _____

Read: Colossians 3:12–14

Therefore, as God's chosen people, holy and dearly loved, clothe yourselves with compassion, kindness, humility, gentleness and patience. Bear with each other and forgive one another if any of you has a grievance against someone. Forgive as the Lord forgave you. And over all these virtues put on love, which binds them all together in perfect unity.

Reflect

Consider the following questions based on the second part of Paul's exhortation to pursue forgiveness by bearing with others.

1. How would I define a *grievance*, as Paul uses it in this passage?

2. Why does Paul connect the ideas of forgiving people and "bearing with" them? When have I found forgiving others to be a burdensome exercise?

3. Does viewing forgiveness as a form of bearing with another person change my attitude toward forgiveness? If so, how?

Receive

In Galatians 6:2, Paul reassures us that as we bear with one another, we cooperate with God's will and ways. He writes, "Carry each other's burdens, and in this way you will fulfill the law of Christ."

How does this promise encourage you to pursue forgiveness today?

Solo Study: Day 3 of 4

What Forgiveness Reflects

Date Completed: _____

Read: Colossians 3:12–14

Therefore, as God's chosen people, holy and dearly loved, clothe yourselves with compassion, kindness, humility, gentleness and patience. Bear with each other and forgive one another if any of you has a grievance against someone. Forgive as the Lord forgave you. And over all these virtues put on love, which binds them all together in perfect unity.

Reflect

Consider the following questions based on the third part of Paul's exhortation to pursue forgiveness by forgiving as God forgives.

1. How would I describe the forgiveness I received from God through faith in Jesus Christ upon surrendering myself to the lordship of Christ?*

---

* If as you move through this Bible study, you realize you have never sincerely and fully surrendered your life to the lordship of Jesus Christ, you can do so right now by praying this straightforward prayer: "Heavenly Father, I know that I am a sinner and that I cannot save myself. By faith I gratefully receive your gift of grace, of salvation, of rescue from the effects of my sin. I am ready to trust your Son, Jesus, as my Lord and Savior, believing that he came to earth as a man, lived a sinless life, died on the cross for my sins, and rose from the dead on the third day. Thank you for forgiving me for my wrongdoing, for adopting me into your family, for transforming me day by day into the likeness of your Son, and for promising me an eternity spent with you. Come into my heart, Lord Jesus! Be my Savior now. In your mighty name I pray. Amen." Please let your group know of your decision so they can celebrate this important day with you!

2. How would I describe the forgiveness I offer to those who have wronged me?

3. What keeps me from more closely reflecting the forgiveness I received from God when I extend forgiveness to another?

Receive

The "Peace Prayer" includes the line, "Where there is offense, let me bring pardon."[3] With that exhortation in mind, spend a few moments in prayer, answering the following three questions before God.

1. What offenses have I been facing recently?
2. What might pardon look like for each?
3. How will God equip me to extend forgiveness for these wrongs?

Solo Study: Day 4 of 4

What Forgiveness Prompts

Date Completed: _____

Read: Colossians 3:12–14

Therefore, as God's chosen people, holy and dearly loved, clothe yourselves with compassion, kindness, humility, gentleness and patience. Bear with each other and forgive one another if any of you has a grievance against someone. Forgive as the Lord forgave you. And over all these virtues put on love, which binds them all together in perfect unity.

Reflect

Consider the following questions based on the fourth and final part of Paul's exhortation to pursue forgiveness by putting on love.

1. In what ways do I see forgiveness as a significant expression of love, as the apostle Paul writes in this passage?

2. When have I tried to forgive another person without loving that person? How did it go?

3. Why does Paul say the cumulative effect of practicing compassion, humility, patience, and forgiveness is unity? How do I see these things fitting together?

Receive

In Psalm 133:1, we read these words: "How good and pleasant it is when God's people live together in unity!"

What other words would you use to mean "good and pleasant"? "Desirable"? "Laudable"? "Beautiful"? Jot them down below, and then thank God that as you go his way instead of your own, prioritizing the things he himself finds valuable, you will be contributing to those very things.

-
-
-
-
-

To prepare for next week's session on awe, please read chapter 10 of *Life-Minded: 8 Practices for Belonging to God and Each Other.*

SESSION 06 INSIGHTS + IDEAS

Session 07

Awe

Session Setup

What stokes a sense of awe for you? A towering, ornate cathedral? The coos of a newborn baby? A stirring symphony? The deep bond you feel with your oldest and dearest friend? Awe is a universal human experience, but for the follower of Jesus, it is a deeply spiritual one as well.

Consider the intricacies of a spring flower or the delicate symmetry of a snowflake, and the beauty of creation can leave you awestruck over the Creator's intention and artistry. And this is as it should be! From a Christian worldview, awe is a form of worship that bubbles up inside of us as we remember that evidences of God's handiwork abound. Moving experiences aren't mere accidents; they're glimpses of the divine. Complexities in nature ask us to come close, to shake our heads in wonder, to acknowledge that we stand in the presence of the holy One, the Source of all that is beautiful and good.

The Bible boasts plentiful examples of awe as an integral aspect of worship, including this one from the psalmist David:

> When I consider your heavens,
>   the work of your fingers,
> the moon and the stars,
>   which you have set in place,
> what is mankind that you are mindful of them,
>   human beings that you care for them?
>   (Psalm 8:3–4)

Here we find needed clarification about the *practice* of awe, for David wasn't moved until he considered. He wasn't awestruck until he placed himself in the path of the stunning divine.

In this session we'll look at where awe is found and whose job it is to keep us awestruck as we make our way through this sometimes soul-squelching life.

Opener

Before you screen this session's video, share your thoughts on the following questions.

If we define *awe* as the worshiping of God's mystery, when was the last time you experienced awe? What were the circumstances, and what was the experience like for you?

● THE JESUS ENCOUNTER: Matthew 17:1–13

The following Bible passage will be read aloud during the video. The text appears here for your reference.

After six days Jesus took with him Peter, James and John the brother of James, and led them up a high mountain by themselves. There he was transfigured before them. His face shone like the sun, and his clothes became as white as the light. Just then there appeared before them Moses and Elijah, talking with Jesus.

Peter said to Jesus, "Lord, it is good for us to be here. If you wish, I will put up three shelters—one for you, one for Moses and one for Elijah."

While he was still speaking, a bright cloud covered them, and a voice from the cloud said, "This is my Son, whom I love; with him I am well pleased. Listen to him!"

When the disciples heard this, they fell facedown to the ground, terrified. But Jesus came and touched them. "Get up," he said. "Don't be afraid." When they looked up, they saw no one except Jesus.

As they were coming down the mountain, Jesus instructed them, "Don't tell anyone what you have seen, until the Son of Man has been raised from the dead."

The disciples asked him, "Why then do the teachers of the law say that Elijah must come first?"

Jesus replied, "To be sure, Elijah comes and will restore all things. But I tell you, Elijah has already come, and they did not recognize him, but have done to him everything they wished. In the same way the Son of Man is going to suffer at their hands." Then the disciples understood that he was talking to them about John the Baptist.

 Video Notes

As you watch the video, log impactful phrases or key takeaways based on the prompts below.

"Everything is awesome"

The God of all creation

Why God demands glory

Where awe is found

Stoking awe on a mundane Monday

Whose job is it?

Take it all in

Say thanks

Awe is better than cynicism

Let your breath be taken away

Group Discussion

Work through the following questions in full group, addressing as many as time and interest permit.

1. Would you say you're easily awestruck? Why or why not?

2. Why does God demand glory? More pointedly, why does he insist on being the one and only direct object of our "awesome" observations, encounters, and experiences?

3. We say that lots of things are "awesome." Food that someone else has prepared. Seeing a favorite band live. Visiting a bucket-list locale. If God longs to be the only "awesome" part of our lives, then what is a better way to describe the lesser things to which we've been directing our "awe"?

Awe is the acknowledgment that God cannot be reduced to theological platitudes or strict codes of moralism. Awe is the awareness that God is bigger and better than we imagine him to be. Awe is the understanding that God has his arms thrown around the universe and holds all things together by a simple act of his will. Awe is the refusal to tame the Lion of the tribe of Judah whenever we're tempted to think we can keep him locked in a cage.

—Life-Minded

4. In *Life-Minded*, I wrote, "I contend that the primary reason we follow God at all is precisely because we *can't* forecast his ways. Who knows what God will do or why he will do it? I don't! And neither do you. We follow not because we've been given the course map but because we know where the finish line sits. It sits at the spot marked *victory*." What do you make of this assertion? When have you found peace in a troubling situation even though you had no clue which step to take next?

5. Thinking back on that situation, why do you suppose God didn't reveal at once all the steps you should take to get from the problem you faced to the solution that ultimately resolved it? Tick any of the statements below that resonate with you.

   ■ *Testing and growth.* "God allowed me to face an unexpected challenge so my faith could be refined and so I could experience deeper spiritual growth."

- *Prevention of complacency.* "God allowed me to be confronted with a situation beyond my control so I would seek his wisdom and guidance with greater diligence."

- *Revelation of God's sovereignty.* "God allowed these circumstances to reinforce my understanding that he is not subject to human expectations or limitations . . . and that his plans are beyond my comprehension."

- *Increased intimacy with God.* "God allowed me to walk through a difficult time so I would draw near to him fervently, resulting in a stronger bond between him and me."

- *Expansion of faith.* "God pushed me outside of my comfort zone, knowing I would have to genuinely trust in his character, his faithfulness, and his love to hold fast to the divine hope I claim."

- _____

  _____

6. In the book of Isaiah, we're reminded that God is *other* than humanity:

   "For my thoughts are not your thoughts,
       neither are your ways my ways,"
           declares the LORD.
   "As the heavens are higher than the earth,
       so are my ways higher than your ways
       and my thoughts than your thoughts." (55:8–9)

   From your (admittedly human!) perspective, what do you see as the drawbacks to following a God who is other than you, whose thoughts and ways are not at all like your own? What are the benefits? Working in pairs, complete the following grid using either firsthand experience and study or the verses provided below the grid. Then, share a few insights with the group.

Perceived Drawbacks	Undeniable Benefits

Reference Verses

- Drawbacks: Job 11:7–9; Proverbs 19:21; Isaiah 45:9; 1 Corinthians 1:25 (yes, this verse may be read as both a benefit and a drawback!); Romans 9:20–21; Psalm 131:1
- Benefits: Romans 11:33; 1 Corinthians 1:25; Proverbs 3:5–6; Romans 8:28; Jeremiah 29:11; Psalm 37:4; Isaiah 26:3

7. How might these drawbacks and benefits facilitate a sense of spiritual awe in your daily life? Note three practical ways below before sharing your thoughts with your group.

1.

2.

3.

Praying It Through

In pairs, consider before God your answers to the following questions, asking God to encourage you in your quest to live more awestruck of his character and activity in the world.

1. In Matthew 17:1–13, the disciples were left undone when they saw Jesus transfigured. They fell to their faces—yes, in terror, but also in awe. How mindful have you been lately of God's awe-inspiring activity in your life? Have you been allowing yourself to be *left undone*?

2. The transfiguration strengthened the faith of Peter, James, and John as it gave them a glimpse into the glorious future that awaited Jesus and reinforced their belief in him as the Messiah. In what ways does your faith need to be strengthened? In what ways do your beliefs need to be reinforced?

3. In instructing his disciples not to tell anyone about what they'd seen, Jesus confirmed the full scope of his mission, which included his crucifixion, resurrection, ascension, and ultimate return. In your own life, how careful are you to keep God's grand plan in mind? Do you allow yourself to be swept away in awe, surrender, and trust as he orchestrates this plan in and through your life? Why or why not?

As you pray, ask God to draw you into his steady presence. Ask him to help you slow your pace so you can reflect earnestly on his mystery, his majesty, his goodness, his care. Ask him to show you something of his character you've never seen before.

Thank him for the gift of awe, of being left undone by a good and glorious God.

The Challenge

Before ending today's session, discuss in full group how last week's challenge went, and then share which of the commitments below you plan to uphold this week.

To prioritize experiencing awe, this week I will . . .

- Spend time in nature by taking a walk in a park, going for a hike in the woods, sitting beside a body of water, or taking in a sunrise or sunset.

- Engage wholeheartedly in worship by attending a service at church or holding a "service" at home, during which I will sing, pray, and meditate earnestly on God's Word.

- Prioritize gratitude each day by seeking out a handful of awe-inspiring things and intentionally thanking God for each.

- Contemplate God's character by reflecting each day on a specific attribute—his mercy, his wisdom, and so on—and pondering how it impacts my life.
- Experience a concert, art exhibit, or cultural performance that evokes a sense of wonder and awe.

- _____

  _____

Note any thoughts or plans in the space below.

Solo Study: Day 1 of 4

Acknowledge God's Majesty

Date Completed: _____

This week, using four different Scripture passages, we will meditate on practices that draw us into awe for God's character and activity in the world.

Read: Psalm 8:3–4

> When I consider your heavens,
>   the work of your fingers,
> the moon and the stars,
>   which you have set in place,
> what is mankind that you are mindful of them,
>   human beings that you care for them?

Reflect

Consider the following questions based on the first passage, Psalm 8:3–4, which leads us to awe by pondering the works of God's hands.

1. Is it my responsibility to stoke a sense of awe in my own spiritual life? Why or why not?

2. When has contemplating the vastness of God's creation, from the heavens to the intricate details of nature, drawn me into a state of awe?

3. What is awe-inspiring about the season I'm in, the setting I'm in, the circumstances I'm in, the view I presently have, the people nearby?

Receive

The Bible says that when we fear God, coming before him in a spirit of reverence and awe, we set in motion many benefits:

- God will confide in us, making his covenant known to us (Psalm 25:14).
- The angel of the Lord will encamp around us (Psalm 34:7).
- We will access knowledge (Proverbs 1:7).
- We will access wisdom and understanding as we follow his precepts (Psalm 111:10).

Which of these promises is most meaningful to you today? Why?

Solo Study: Day 2 of 4

Reflect on God's Attributes

Date Completed: _____

Read: Isaiah 40:28

> Do you not know?
>   Have you not heard?
> The LORD is the everlasting God,
>   the Creator of the ends of the earth.
> He will not grow tired or weary,
>   and his understanding no one can fathom.

Reflect

Consider the following questions based on the second passage, Isaiah 40:28, which leads us to awe by contemplating God's attributes.

1. What difference does it make in my life that I serve a God who is *omnipresent*—all present?

2. What difference does it make in my life that I serve a God who is *omniscient*—all knowing?

3. What difference does it make in my life that I serve a God who is *omnipotent*—all powerful?

Receive

God longs to bless his children with the divine resources of his presence, his perspective, his power. Let the following verses remind you of these truths.

> So do not fear, for I am with you;
>> do not be dismayed, for I am your God.
> I will strengthen you and help you;
>> I will uphold you with my righteous right hand.
>> (Isaiah 41:10)

> God is our refuge and strength,
>> an ever-present help in trouble.
> Therefore we will not fear, though the earth give
>> way
> and the mountains fall into the heart of the sea,
> though its waters roar and foam
>> and the mountains quake with their surging.
>> (Psalm 46:1–3)

> Come to me, all you who are weary and burdened, and I will give you rest. Take my yoke upon you and learn from me, for I am gentle and humble in heart, and you will find rest for your souls. For my yoke is easy and my burden is light. (Matthew 11:28–30)

If any of you lacks wisdom, you should ask God, who gives generously to all without finding fault, and it will be given to you. (James 1:5)

Praise be to the God and Father of our Lord Jesus Christ, the Father of compassion and the God of all comfort, who comforts us in all our troubles, so that we can comfort those in any trouble with the comfort we ourselves receive from God. (2 Corinthians 1:3–4)

Solo Study: Day 3 of 4
Praise God

Date Completed: _____

Read: Psalm 95:6

> Come, let us bow down in worship,
>   let us kneel before the LORD our Maker.

Reflect

Consider the following questions based on the third passage, Psalm 95:6, which leads us to awe by worshiping our God.

1. Figuratively speaking, what does it mean for me to "bow down in worship" before God?

2. When was the last time I *literally* bowed down in worship before God? How is my heart's posture toward him changed when my body's posture shifts?

3. Why was bowing down the typical reaction of those who encountered God's presence throughout Scripture?

Receive

In Matthew 2:10–11 we read of the wise men making their way to find the Christ child after learning that the Messiah had finally been born: "When they saw the star, they were overjoyed. On coming to the house, they saw the child with his mother Mary, and they bowed down and worshiped him. Then they opened their treasures and presented him with gifts of gold, frankincense and myrrh."

What do you notice about their reflexive reactions to encountering Jesus?

Solo Study: Day 4 of 4

Seek a Reverent Heart

Date Completed: _____

Read: Proverbs 9:10

> The fear of the LORD is the beginning of wisdom,
>   and knowledge of the Holy One is
>   understanding.

Reflect

Consider the following questions based on the fourth and final passage, Proverbs 9:10, which leads us to awe by fearing the Lord.

1. What kind of "wisdom," "knowledge," and "understanding" is the writer of Proverbs referring to here? What words would I use to define each?

wisdom

knowledge

understanding

2. When have I tried to obtain wisdom apart from "fearing" (or revering) the Lord? How did things turn out for me?

3. What is a nugget of wisdom I have gained only as a result of fearing or revering God?

Receive

If you have been in corporate worship settings for some time, you've probably come across the oft-sung hymn "Holy, Holy, Holy," written by Reginald Heber, a nineteenth-century Anglican bishop. Spend a few minutes meditating on his lyrics below, which compel the reverent heart to direct its energies toward God.

> Holy, holy, holy! Lord God Almighty!
> Early in the morning our song shall rise to thee;
> holy, holy, holy, merciful and mighty!
> God in three persons, blessed Trinity!
>
> Holy, holy, holy! All the saints adore thee,
> casting down their golden crowns around the
> glassy sea;
> cherubim and seraphim, falling down before thee,
> who was, and is, and evermore shall be.

To prepare for next week's session on grace, please read chapter 11 of *Life-Minded: 8 Practices for Belonging to God and Each Other.*

SESSION 07 INSIGHTS + IDEAS

—————————— Session 08 ——————————

Grace

Grace, grace, amazing grace! If you are a follower of Jesus, it's likely you can't read or say the word *grace* without grinning. Why? Because both our present faith and our future hope rest on the singular concept of God's grace.

Grace is God's unmerited favor offered freely to humanity and is the undisputed cornerstone of Christian salvation. Grace is the conduit for sinners to receive forgiveness for their sin, redemption, and life both now and forever with God. As such, grace is the single most powerful gift we can give to another person. It's an introduction to the One who stands willing, ready, and able to rescue them from the consequences of their wretchedness and sin.

In the Sermon on the Mount, Jesus affirms that as his followers we are to extend to others the same grace we have received: "For if you forgive other people when they sin against you, your heavenly Father will also forgive you. But if you do not forgive others their sins, your Father will not forgive your sins" (Matthew 6:14–15). In other words, we are to release others from the results of their sin as we have been divinely released from ours. Why? Because forgiving others for their wrongdoing is the first step in positioning ourselves to be *gracious* toward them, to be conduits of God's grace in their lives. It is only by grace—our receiving God's grace *and* our passing along that grace to others—that the unity we seek can unfold.

The power of giving grace lies in its transformative effect on individuals and relationships. When we choose to show grace to others,

158

we break the cycle of resentment and hostility, which in turn has the power to heal wounds, mend broken relationships, and bring about the reconciliation our world so desperately needs.

But what does it look like in our vitriolic modern-day society to give grace? Is it even appropriate to do such a thing given our present state of disunity? How do we know if people want this grace we so dearly prize? We'll talk about these issues and more in this session on our eighth and final practice, *giving grace.*

Opener

Before you screen this session's video, share your thoughts on the following questions.

When have you given something to someone that they neither deserved nor could repay?

What happened after you made your gracious offering?

● THE JESUS ENCOUNTER: John 8:2–11

The following Bible passage will be read aloud during the video. The text appears here for your reference.

At dawn he appeared again in the temple courts, where all the people gathered around him, and he sat down to teach them. The teachers of the law and the Pharisees brought in a woman caught in adultery. They made her stand before the group and said to Jesus,

"Teacher, this woman was caught in the act of adultery. In the Law Moses commanded us to stone such women. Now what do you say?" They were using this question as a trap, in order to have a basis for accusing him.

But Jesus bent down and started to write on the ground with his finger. When they kept on questioning him, he straightened up and said to them, "Let any one of you who is without sin be the first to throw a stone at her." Again he stooped down and wrote on the ground.

At this, those who heard began to go away one at a time, the older ones first, until only Jesus was left, with the woman still standing there. Jesus straightened up and asked her, "Woman, where are they? Has no one condemned you?"

"No one, sir," she said.

"Then neither do I condemn you," Jesus declared. "Go now and leave your life of sin."

 Video Notes

As you watch the video, log impactful phrases or key takeaways based on the prompts below.

Talking about God with your heart surgeon

The joy of spiritual dialogue

Walk toward the weirdness

Believers believe

Believers help others believe

Absolutely true good news

"Has no one condemned you?"

Safety, connection, purpose

Your ready yes

Swimming in oceans of grace

Group Discussion

Work through the following questions in full group, addressing as many as time and interest permit.

1. Which element of the video resonated most with you, and why?

2. Put yourself in the shoes of the woman Jesus forgave in John 8:2–11. As she responded to his question, "Has no one condemned you?" with the simple phrase, "No one, sir," what emotions do you imagine she was feeling? Why?

   When have you been left similarly undone by the kindness of Christ in your daily life?

3. What thoughts, attitudes, or even actions toward others are prompted in you as you sit with the image of the adulterous woman being graciously regarded by Jesus, and with the memory of you yourself being received in this manner by Christ?

As you and I encounter wayward people in our day-to-day lives, I wonder what percent of our time and energy we spend being frustrated with their waywardness and what percent we spend watching and waiting, hoping beyond hope that they'll come home.

—*Life-Minded*

In accordance with the example set by Jesus, a straightforward way to think about how to give grace to others is by contrasting the concept of grace with the concepts of justice and mercy:

- Justice is getting what we deserve.
- Mercy is *not* getting what we deserve.
- Grace is getting what we *don't* deserve.

4. Look up and read aloud Romans 6:23. What does the apostle Paul say it would have looked like for God to give us *justice* when we found ourselves in need of salvation?

5. Look up and read aloud Romans 5:8. What does Paul say it looked like for God to give us *mercy* even while we were still sinners?

6. Look up and read aloud Romans 5:20–21. What does Paul say it looks like for us to receive *grace* when we faced certain spiritual death for our sin?

7. Read the quote in the sidebar. How might the lavish offering of grace to people who are struggling accomplish the purpose of unity we've been considering throughout this study?

Literally, *gospel* means "good news." And if there's one thing our world needs today, a little good news has to be it. People I come across are dying for good news. They are burdened by the poor decisions they've made—the affair, the abortion, the money they stole. The weight of sin crushes their soul, and they don't know how to get free. Jesus is how they get free. Jesus is how they find hope. Jesus is how they move forward. Jesus is how they live.

—*Life-Minded*

---

8. In John 1:16, we read of God that "out of his fullness we have all received grace in place of grace already given." Why does it matter that God's grace is abundant, that it keeps pouring into the lives of those who long for it, that it never will run out?

Praying It Through

In pairs, consider before God your answers to the following questions, asking God to encourage you in your quest to live more graciously toward the people you come across.

1. Have you been approaching people lately with an initial posture of acceptance, eager to reflect the kindness and love of Jesus, regardless of their willingness to engage with you?

2. Do you tend to be critical of others' mistakes and judge them (even silently) for their misdeeds, or are you quick to extend a spirit or word of compassion, recognizing that you too make mistakes?

3. Is love at the core of your actions and interactions? Do you strive to love others unconditionally, in the same way God loves you?

In Proverbs 11:25, King Solomon writes, "A generous person will prosper; whoever refreshes others will be refreshed." As you pray, ask God to focus your attention on this distinctly unifying aspect of graciousness.

Thank him for setting the bar at *grace* with us . . . not merely at *mercy*, certainly not at *justice*. Thank him for demonstrating through the actions and reactions of his Son, Jesus, how to live graciously here and now.

The Challenge

Before ending today's session, discuss in full group how last week's challenge went, and then share which of the commitments below you plan to uphold this week.

To prioritize the practice of giving grace, this week I will . . .

- Greet people I would normally breeze past with a smile and even a kind word.
- Refrain from passing judgment on others, seeking first to understand their perspective and circumstances before forming opinions about them.
- Practice patience with others' shortcomings, remembering that God remains patient with me as I move through life imperfectly.
- Celebrate others' successes by rejoicing in their achievements instead of being envious of them.
- Give the benefit of the doubt, assuming the best of others' intentions when their words or actions (or lack thereof) are unclear.
- Ask for feedback, requesting constructive input from people who can help me grow in graciousness.
- Share the gospel with someone when the opportunity to have a spiritual conversation presents itself.

- _____

_____

Note any thoughts or plans in the space below.

Before You Dismiss

Since this marks the end of your formal time together as a *Life-Minded* group, consider taking a few moments before you head out to reflect and comment on one or two of the following prompts:

- The practice (devotion, curiosity, discernment, peace, service, forgiveness, awe, or grace) that was most convicting or compelling to me was . . .
- The end-of-session challenge I'm proudest to have completed was . . .
- The passage of Scripture that struck me most profoundly was . . .
- The group discussion I found most stimulating was . . .
- The realization I'll remember for quite some time is . . .
- The aspect of spiritual growth from this study I feel most grateful for is . . .
- The facet of unity in my life that I hope is most evident to others as I go forward from this study is . . .

Following this final discussion, if it makes sense for your group, establish a group text or other communication channel for checking in with each other next week regarding how this session's challenge went for you.

Solo Study: Day 1 of 4
Focus on God's Love

Date Completed: _____

This week, we will meditate on four aspects of elevating the practice of giving grace in our lives by looking to the apostle Paul's words in Ephesians 2:4–9.

Read: Ephesians 2:4–9

But because of his great love for us, God, who is rich in mercy, made us alive with Christ even when we were dead in transgressions—it is by grace you have been saved. And God raised us up with Christ and seated us with him in the heavenly realms in Christ Jesus, in order that in the coming ages he might show the incomparable riches of his grace, expressed in his kindness to us in Christ Jesus. For it is by grace you have been saved, through faith—and this is not from yourselves, it is the gift of God—not by works, so that no one can boast.

Reflect

Consider the following questions based on the first part of Paul's injunction to give grace because of God's great love for us.

1. How would I put my own words to what Paul means by describing God's love as "great" in the first line of this passage?

2. What difference does it make knowing that God's gift of grace to me is rooted not in my worthiness or in his frustration over having to "cover" for me but only in his *great love for me*?

3. What can I take away from God's grace-giving model about how to give grace to the people I come across?

Receive

Read the following verses aloud, turning them into a prayer to God. How great is God's love for you! Soak in that truth now.

> So, what do you think? With God on our side like this, how can we lose? If God didn't hesitate to put everything on the line for us, embracing our condition and exposing himself to the worst by sending his own Son, is there anything else he wouldn't gladly and freely do for us? And who would dare tangle with God by messing with one of God's chosen? Who would dare even to point a finger? The One who died for us—who was raised to life for us!—is in the presence of God at this very moment sticking up for us. Do you think anyone is going to be able to drive a wedge between us and Christ's love for us? There is no way! Not trouble, not hard times, not hatred, not hunger, not homelessness, not bullying threats, not backstabbing, not even the worst sins listed in Scripture:

> They kill us in cold blood because they hate
>   you.
> We're sitting ducks; they pick us off one by
>   one.

None of this fazes us because Jesus loves us. I'm absolutely convinced that nothing—nothing living or dead, angelic or demonic, today or tomorrow, high or low, thinkable or unthinkable—absolutely *nothing* can get between us and God's love because of the way that Jesus our Master has embraced us. (Romans 8:31–39 MSG)

Solo Study: Day 2 of 4

Focus on Your Salvation

Date Completed: _____

Read: Ephesians 2:4–9

But because of his great love for us, God, who is rich in mercy, made us alive with Christ even when we were dead in transgressions—it is by grace you have been saved. And God raised us up with Christ and seated us with him in the heavenly realms in Christ Jesus, in order that in the coming ages he might show the incomparable riches of his grace, expressed in his kindness to us in Christ Jesus. For it is by grace you have been saved, through faith—and this is not from yourselves, it is the gift of God—not by works, so that no one can boast.

Reflect

Consider the following questions based on the second part of Paul's injunction to give grace because of our salvation in Christ.

1. What did my life look like when I was "dead in transgressions"?

2. How did I come to encounter and accept God's gift of grace?

3. When was the last time I shared my spiritual before-and-after story with someone who doesn't know Christ?

Receive

When you practice giving grace, treating others in the same way God has treated you, Luke 6:35 says that you are positioning yourself for great spiritual benefit. Let Jesus's words minister to you today: "But love your enemies, do good to them, and lend to them without expecting to get anything back. Then your reward will be great, and you will be children of the Most High, because he is kind to the ungrateful and wicked."

Solo Study: Day 3 of 4

Focus on Jesus's Exaltation

Date Completed: _____

Read: Ephesians 2:4–9

But because of his great love for us, God, who is rich in mercy, made us alive with Christ even when we were dead in transgressions—it is by grace you have been saved. And God raised us up with Christ and seated us with him in the heavenly realms in Christ Jesus, in order that in the coming ages he might show the incomparable riches of his grace, expressed in his kindness to us in Christ Jesus. For it is by grace you have been saved, through faith—and this is not from yourselves, it is the gift of God—not by works, so that no one can boast.

Reflect

Consider the following questions based on the third part of Paul's injunction to give grace because of the incomparable riches of God's grace.

1. What does it mean to me to be "raised up" with Christ?

2. How does understanding that the future has been secured for me in Christ Jesus embolden me to face the challenges of today?

3. What does this passage say is God's posture toward me as he extends to me his offer of grace?

Receive

Refresh your imagination with what Scripture says is our future destination in Christ Jesus by reading the following passage and then journaling a prayer of thanksgiving to God.

> And I heard a loud voice from the throne saying, "Look! God's dwelling place is now among the people, and he will dwell with them. They will be his people, and God himself will be with them and be their God. 'He will wipe every tear from their eyes. There will be no more death' or mourning or crying or pain, for the old order of things has passed away." (Revelation 21:3–4)

Solo Study: Day 4 of 4

Focus on Faith

Date Completed: _____

Read: Ephesians 2:4–9

But because of his great love for us, God, who is rich in mercy, made us alive with Christ even when we were dead in transgressions—it is by grace you have been saved. And God raised us up with Christ and seated us with him in the heavenly realms in Christ Jesus, in order that in the coming ages he might show the incomparable riches of his grace, expressed in his kindness to us in Christ Jesus. For it is by grace you have been saved, through faith—and this is not from yourselves, it is the gift of God—not by works, so that no one can boast.

Reflect

Consider the following questions based on the fourth and final part of Paul's injunction to give grace because our faith is a gift from God.

1. When did I finally accept the fact that no matter how many good works I racked up, they would never be enough to satisfy God's standard of perfection?

2. Why did God wipe away good works as a viable means for satisfying him? What was he protecting me from?

3. How do the following verses build on Ephesians 2:4–9 to show me the purposes of good works, given that they can't secure my salvation in Christ?

Matthew 5:16

Galatians 5:13

Ephesians 2:10

Ephesians 4:12

1 Peter 2:12

Grace | 177

Receive

Saint Augustine once wrote, "Grace is given, not because we have done good works, but in order that we may be able to do them."[4]

How does understanding grace not as a reward for good works but as a source of empowerment to perform them shape your perspective on your actions toward others today?

SESSION 08 INSIGHTS + IDEAS

Tips for Facilitating Your Small Group

Thank you for facilitating a *Life-Minded* group!

If you have been walking with Jesus for any length of time, then you've probably already discovered that what he said about it being more of a blessing to give than to receive (Acts 20:35) is absolutely, unequivocally true. Because you have raised your hand and made yourself available to serve your group by facilitating your time together, you will be rewarded in unique ways.

This is how life with Christ works.

At the same time, it's important to acknowledge that your investment of time, energy, commitment, prayer, and concern is a *weighty* one. Be sure to carve out sufficient resources—both on your calendar and in your heart—to fill this role.

Once you are ready to jump in spiritually, emotionally, and practically, make sure you work through the following guidelines and tips prior to your first group meeting. Allow enough time (ideally six weeks) for you to recruit your group and for your group members to secure their workbooks, prepare for the study, and read through the first three chapters of *Life-Minded: 8 Practices for Belonging to God and Each Other* (Our Daily Bread 2024) if desired.

Group Selection and Scheduling

This study is intended to be experienced not on your own but in the context of a group.

If you don't already have a group to work through this content with, consider inviting six to eight people from your church, neighborhood, friend group, or extended family to join you.

Prior to your first group meeting, designate the nine dates when you will be meeting so group members can plan for faithful participation. Once per week for nine consecutive weeks is best. The first meeting covers the introductory session and allows for group members to get to know each other before getting into the eight practices at the heart of *Life-Minded*.

Session Themes

In this nine-session experience, which focuses on eight practices for prioritizing unity with greater intention, you and your group members will be asked to engage with the following concepts:

- Being chronically distracted with the things of the world versus living fully devoted to God

- Engaging with others from a posture of assumption versus a posture of curiosity

- Using our words to tear others down versus using our words to build them up

- In pridefulness canceling people who wrong us versus in humility canceling the rage we feel toward them

- Indulging self-centeredness to lord our power over others versus squelching self-centeredness to serve them

- Harboring resentment and holding grudges versus harboring love and forgiving others

- Contributing to the plague of brutality in our world versus contributing to the beauty that always exists

- Exacting justice when others do wrong versus lavishing wrongdoers with the same grace we have received from God (since we're wrongdoers too!)

Each session includes Bible study, robust group discussions, corporate prayer, and occasions between sessions for self-reflection, repentance, and spiritual growth. Through this experience, you will deepen your appreciation for the fact that we have the same power living within us that "raised Christ from the dead and seated him in the place of honor at God's right hand in the heavenly realms" (Ephesians 1:20 NLT). Together we can participate in God's good work in the world, which always is aimed at redemption, restoration, and renewal . . . at a grand *reunification*, if you will.

Session Structure

Except for the introductory session, which only provides about sixty minutes of structured content, each session is intended to run for ninety minutes (plus any fellowship time before or afterward) and is made up of seven segments:

Element	Duration	Purpose
Session Setup	5m	A narrative overview of the session's theme, to be read aloud by a group member to orient the group to the topic at hand.
Opener	10m	One or two provocative, theme-related questions for the full group to answer prior to diving into the session's video.
The Jesus Encounter	n/a	The primary Scripture passage from the Gospels on which the session is based. Note that no time is reserved for the reading of this passage; either the verses will be read aloud during the video, or a group member will be asked to read them aloud during the Group Discussion segment.
Video Notes	15m	Brief prompts for note-taking during the screening of the video teaching (12–16 minutes, depending on the session).

Element	Duration	Purpose
Group Discussion	40m	Robust discussion questions and activities to help group members interact with the session's theme and video content.
Praying It Through	10m	Three self-reflective questions for group members to address in pairs, framing their answers as prayer requests to God.
The Challenge	10m	Engaging and approachable options for practicing the session's theme before the group meets again. Blank space follows each Challenge segment for idea capturing. These options complement the end-of-chapter challenges in the book *Life-Minded* without regurgitating them verbatim. Note: For sessions 2–8, time should be reserved at the beginning of each Challenge segment to hear group members report on how the previous week's challenge went for them. (There is no previous week's challenge for the introductory session or session 1.)
	Total: 90m	

The duration of each segment is a general estimate. While these estimates can help structure your time together, the needs of your group, and the discussions that arise each week, may lead you to use your time differently.

Between group sessions, participants are to complete four fifteen-minute Solo Study sessions, which encourage them to prioritize that week's practice as they *read* a passage of Scripture, *reflect* on the reading by answering two to four questions, and *receive* encouragement from the Bible or a Christian saint of old. Group members are also asked to read the chapter of *Life-Minded* that pairs with the next week's theme.

Preparing for Group Sessions

In your role as facilitator, be sure to tend to the following tasks prior to each session.

Gather Materials

Prior to your first group meeting, be sure each member has the following materials ready to go:

- A copy of this study guide
- A copy of *Life-Minded: 8 Practices for Belonging to God and Each Other* (Our Daily Bread Publishing 2024)
- A pen
- A Bible (this guide primarily cites the New International Version, but any translation will do)

You will also need access to the videos that support each of the nine sessions. QR codes can be found in the Video Notes segment within each session in this guide. Be sure you're able to pull up each video on either a TV or laptop for easier viewing by the full group. You can access the videos by computer using the following URLs:

Introductory Session: go.odb.org/lifeminded-introduction

Session 01—Devotion: go.odb.org/lifeminded-session1

Session 02—Curiosity: go.odb.org/lifeminded-session2

Session 03—Discernment: go.odb.org/lifeminded-session3

Session 04—Peace: go.odb.org/lifeminded-session4

Session 05—Service: go.odb.org/lifeminded-session5

Session 06—Forgiveness: go.odb.org/lifeminded-session6

Session 07—Awe: go.odb.org/lifeminded-session7

Session 08—Grace: go.odb.org/lifeminded-session8

Preview the Session

Orient yourself to the session's content prior to each meeting so you're not coming to the gathering cold. To that end, consider these practices:

- Reading through the entire session, highlighting the discussion questions you want to be sure to save time to address.
- Answering the discussion questions ahead of time, so if conversation is slow to unfold, you can offer your thoughtful perspective first.
- Asking God to guide your thoughts and to put apt words on your tongue as you facilitate your group. He knows what every person in the group is going through and what words, inputs, and discussions will best minister to them.

Ready Your Heart

To maximize your group's time together, commit to spending thirty to forty-five minutes each week preparing not just your materials but your *heart*. This might include these practices:

- Reading the broader context surrounding each Bible reference and noting insights you might bring up during group discussion.
- Reaching out to each group member by text or phone call to offer a word of encouragement and to solicit prayer requests.
- Praying for each group member by name.

Facilitating Group Sessions

During your group's meetings, you will need to take the lead in managing the clock, various group dynamics, and the overall mood. What follows are a dozen tried-and-true tips you might find useful as you work to keep things moving ahead.

1. *Keep time.* Consider designating a timekeeper who will subtly cue you when it's time to move to the next activity or segment. The timekeeper can find allotted times for each segment in the table on pages 181–82.

2. *Gauge participants' comfort level with reading aloud.* There are several segments that are to be read aloud each week. Note that not everyone is comfortable reading aloud. Check in with your group members privately before the first session to inquire about their comfort level with reading or praying aloud.

3. *Listen well.* Listen more than you talk. Ask follow-up questions whenever group members share poignant insights. Take notes on what people say so you can reflect on your time together between sessions.

4. *Balance personalities.* Invariably your group will have members who are more comfortable expressing their thoughts and opinions than others. Be careful to (thoughtfully, gently) draw out quiet members and to (tenderly, compassionately) help more exuberant members practice passing the figurative mic. For quieter types, you might say something such as, "Jane, if you're okay sharing your thoughts on this question, I'll circle back to you after we hear from a few others." Then follow up with Jane after two or three others have answered to see if she is willing to chime in. For more talkative members, you could say something like, "All right, who else can relate to what John is saying?" This gives you the opportunity to invite discussion from others.

5. *Wait for eight.* Depending on the day, the question at hand, and the personalities involved, you may pose a question that nobody answers. Before you jump in to rescue the situation, wait a full eight seconds. Yes, it will feel like an eternity. But it will be the patient pause some participants need before they are ready to speak.

6. *Resolve interruptions.* On the other end of the spectrum from the previous point, you will invariably hit upon topics for which everyone is *eager* to share her or his opinion. There will be times when the collective enthusiasm for a topic causes people to talk over each other. When this happens, try to keep tabs on who was interrupted so that as the conversation settles, you can come back around and say, "Allison and Mike, I think you both had thoughts on this question. Can we hear from each of you in turn?"

7. *Accept all input.* It takes courage to speak up in a group setting. Be sure to offer encouragement each time a member shares. Afterward, say, "Thank you for sharing your insights."

8. *Allow for cross-group talk.* During group discussion, encourage participants to respond to each other without "going through" you each time.

9. *Practice cross-session weaving.* If you take good notes each week, it will be easy to refer back to insights made during previous sessions, so your group can start to tie together the various concepts they encounter during this nine-session experience.

10. *Be satisfied with a sampling.* You don't need to hear from every member in response to every question. If one or two people share their thoughts on a specific item and you're ready to move on, go ahead and move on.

11. *Leverage the offline option.* If a conversation is veering off topic, confidently table the discussion for later. Say something like, "While this conversation is fascinating, I'm getting the stink eye from our beloved timekeeper. We'd better move on."

12. *Hold fast to hope.* This study touches on some deep-seated issues, which may cause certain discussions to feel heavy or hard. Don't be afraid of what's real. But also be sure to hold fast to hope and to present an optimistic perspective each week.

Note: While confidentiality is important for fostering an atmosphere where participants feel comfortable sharing, in the event that a group member confides to you that he or she is in an abusive situation, in danger from others or from self-harm, or has witnessed abusive or criminal activity, report this immediately to your pastoral and/or local authorities, as appropriate.

Remember that the goal of small-group discussion is to create a safe and supportive space for participants to share ideas, learn from one another, and deepen their understanding of the topic. Your effective facilitation enhances the overall experience and promotes productive and enriching conversation, so thank you for thoughtfully and prayerfully filling this critical role.

Notes

1. Merriam-Webster, s.v. "devotion," accessed February 28, 2024, https://www.merriam-webster.com/dictionary /devotion.
2. Augustine of Hippo, "Sermon 69," in *Patrologiae Cursus Completus*, ed. Jacques-Paul Migne, vol. 38, *Augustinus Hipponensis* (Paris: Apud Garnier Frates, 1865), 441.
3. "Peace Prayer," *La Clochette*, December 1912.
4. Augustine of Hippo, *On the Spirit and the Letter*, trans. W. J. Sparrow Simpson (New York: The McMillan Co., 1925), 53.

Spread the Word
by Doing One Thing.

- Give a copy of this book as a gift.
- Share the QR code link via your social media.
- Write a review of this book on your blog, favorite bookseller's website, or at ODB.org/store.
- Recommend this book to your church, small group, or book club.

Connect with us. [f] [o]

Our Daily Bread Publishing
PO Box 3566, Grand Rapids, MI 49501, USA
Email: books@odb.org

Love God. Love Others.

with 🌾 Our Daily Bread.

Your gift changes lives.

Connect with us. 🅕 📷

Our Daily Bread Publishing
PO Box 3566, Grand Rapids, MI 49501, USA
Email: books@odb.org